The Bulgarian Air Force
In World War II
Germany´s Forgotten Ally

Dedicated to:
Marisol (my life), my parents (Salud y Eduardo), Merce, Caco, June, Iñigo, Ibón, Walin and Manuel Luis (Yoyo).

Thanks to:
Dimitar Nedialkov for his help in the first steps of the work and for making my interest in bulgarian aviation grow; Stephan Boshniakov for his help with the pictures, Georgi from bibliotekata, tod from Rathbonemuseum, José Antonio Muñoz Molero for his friendship and efforts and Ricardo Ramallo Gil for his invaluable help always.

EDUARDO M. GIL MARTÍNEZ

The Bulgarian Air Force In World War II
Germany´s Forgotten Ally

KAGERO

FIRST EDITION
© by KAGERO Publishing, 2017

AUTHOR
Eduardo M. Gil Martínez

EDITORS
Eduardo M. Gil Martínez

TRANSLATION/PROOFREADING
José Antonio Muñoz Molero/Tomasz Basarabowicz

COVER
Łukasz Maj

DTP
Kagero Studio

COLOR PROFILES
Color profiles: Arkadiusz Wróbel, Janusz Światłoń

PHOTO SOURCE
Public Domain, Kagero Archives, Bundesarchiv. Courtesy of: Stephan Boshniakov,
Carmel Attard, Rod´s Warbird, ASISBIZ, Georgi from Bibliotekata, Fernando Salobral,
Tod Rathbone (rathbonemuseum.com)

ISBN 978-83-65437-55-6

DISTRIBUTION
Kagero Publishing
ul. Akacjowa 100, os. Borek, Turka, 20-258 Lublin 62, Poland
phone +48 601-602-056, phone/fax +48 81 501-21-05
e-mail: marketing@kagero.pl
www.kagero.pl

Contents

Preface...7

Chapter I
History of Bulgaria in WW2...9

Chapter II
History of the Bulgarian Air Force (BAF)..13
    1920–1930...13
    1930–1938...14
    1939...17
    1940..20
    1941..23
    1942..31
    1943..32
    1944..36
    1945..39

Chapter III
Fighter Units 41
    Summer 1939...41
    Spring 1941 42
    1942..42
    1 August 1943...42
    12 August 1943...46
    21 October 1943..46
    Systemic bombing of Sofia 46
    14 November 1943..47
    24 November 1943..48
    10 December 1943 48
    20 December 1943 49
    4 January 1944..50
    10 January 1944..51
    24 January 1944..52
    30 March 44...52
    4 April 1944..55
    5 April 1944..55
    Remaining Days Of April 1944...55
    5 May 1944...57

18 May 1944...57
11 June 1944 58
12 June 1944 58
23 June 1944 59
24 June 1944 59
28 June 1944 59
15 July 1944...60
22 July1944..60
10 August 1944..60
17 August 1944..61
26 August 1944..61
Evaluation of BAF Fighter Forces...62
Bulgarian change of side...63
September 1944...63
November..64
January 1945 64

Chapter IV
Bomber units 67

Chapter V
Attack Units 73

Chapter VI
Reconnaisance and Liaison Units..79

Chapter VII
Training Units...85

Chapter VIII
Maritime Surveillance Units..89

Chapter IX
Transport Units...95

Chapter X
Bulgarian Aviation Insignia..99

Chapter XI
Aerial Victory Scoring System of the BAF And Aces 101

Chapter XII
Rank Equivalents In The Bulgarian Air Force...103

Conclusion 105
Bibliography...107

Preface

The activities of the German Air Force – the Luftwaffe – during World War II is well known by those interested in this conflict, due to the large number of works dealing with it. Much less well-known are the air forces of Germany´s allied countries, although in the last few years excellent works have appeared about these too. Among them, perhaps the least known and treated is the Bulgarian Air Force (although its exact name would be Royal Bulgarian Air Force) because of its lesser degree of participation in the war unlike other countries like Hungary, Romania or Finland. That is the reason why the Bulgarian Air Force is Germany´s forgotten ally. Thanks to the excellent work done by the No 1 expert in the matter, Dimitar Nedialkov, the History of Bulgarian aviation in this period has come to light in recent years. Another very important work that enlightened us about the matter since 2000 is "In the Skies of Europe" by Hans W. Neulen, as important was the work by Stephan Boshniakov and Petko Mandjukov; but there were no other outstanding works in English language about Bulgarian Air Force in World War II.

In this text we have sought information from different sources in order to write an account that deals with the different branches of Bulgarian aviation (not only fighters but also bombers, transports, and so on), so we will try to explain the scope of the Bulgarian intervention in World War II on the side of the Germans, although without fighting their Slavic "brothers" from the USSR, which motivated a genuine diplomatic balance impossible to face by the Bulgarian Government. Although the aforementioned works of essential reading on the subject of Mr. Nedialkov, Mr. Boshniakov and Mr. Neulen are the most recommended ones on Bulgarian aviation in the two first cases and the aviation of the Axis countries in the third one, and they have formed the basis of the text; a search has been necessary in dozens of sources to try to complete the research and offer it in the most definitive way.

Despite Bulgaria's geographical location far from the front line, the participation of Bulgarian aviation did not cease during the years of the armed conflict. Initially focused on the control of the new annexed territories and coastal areas so important for the transit of the Axis ships, then to defend their airspace from the waves of Allied bombers who used Bulgaria as an access route to the Romanian oil fields in Ploiesti. Finally after the change of side, the Bulgarians would use their diminished air forces against their previous German ally.

Using various documents about Bulgarian aviation following mainly the works of Mr. Nedialkov, Mr. Neulen, Mr. Boshniakov, Mr. Mandjukov, Mr. Safarík and Mr. Muchovsky, we have been able to create a text that brings us closer to knowing the true potential of the Bulgarian Air Force during World War II; and to know the courage that the Bulgarian airmen demonstrated in their struggle against overwhelmingly superior enemies.

This text serves as a tribute and as a reminder of these women and men immersed in a confrontation whose consequences marked the course of the next 45 years in the country's history.

CHAPTER I

History of Bulgaria in WW2

The history of the kingdom of Bulgaria during World War II was like that of most of the allies that the Germans had in Europe – very complicated. Bulgaria was a German ally during the First World War, and as such, one of those defeated and humiliated by the conditions of surrender accepted. Ethnically and historical Bulgarian territories in Thrace and Macedonia were simply lost. The discontent (as happened in the defeated nations in the Great War) led to the emergence of a growing popular response closer to the right that led them to move closer to an emerging and reactionary Germany.

Bulgaria had to strike a balance between Germany and the Western Powers like France and United Kingdom, which succeeded in having the Bulgarian king declare the neutrality of his country at the beginning of the world conflict on 16 September 1939. Although the war completely altered the influence of these countries, since the rapid fall of France and the takeover of neutral Belgium showed Boris that little could oppose his country against any interference that the Germans decided to have in their country. But the Germans preferred a political approach by advancing with the Soviet movements with the same purpose of approach with their Slavic brothers of Bulgaria, that had its success when in 1940 they pressed Romania to sign the Treaty of Craiova (7 September of 1940) that obliged Romanian to return the region of southern Dobrudja (the coastal region between the mouth of the Danube and the city of Varna, which had been lost even before World War I, since this occurred in 1913 in the context of the Balkan Wars). After this Treaty, Bulgarian cavalry and infantry units mainly took possession of their new territories without conflict, although this is reasonable because the recent Bulgarian past of the area.

But the Reich wanted more from its Bulgarian friend and even began to work diplomatically to join the Axis (the "Tripartite Pact" signed on September 27, 1940 between Germany, Italy and Japan), with a large offer. Since its joining, it would enable Bulgaria to re-drew its present borders to those accepted in the "Treaty of San Stefano" (signed in 1878 and which gave Bulgaria the bulk of Macedonia and Thrace), or what has been considered in denominating Greater Bulgaria. As early as November, King Boris had to travel to Germany to discuss with Adolf Hitler his possible entry into the Axis. But he did not have among his ideas to accede to German desires easily so he tried to delay it with various motivations, in spite of the concern of not being able to maintain his neutral status will always be in his mind.

The plot become more and more entangled, as the Soviets persisted in trying to "control" that area of the Balkans, so they did not hesitate to promise the Bulgarians their support for the Bulgarian claim to Greek Thrace and much of European Turkey. These movements of Moscow were supported from inside Bulgaria by the communist party of this country that took advantage of the proximity between both Slavic countries.

The situation became unsustainable for King Boris, the pressures from Soviets and Germans would finally force him to make a decision, which evidently would not like anything to the despised part and that would bring its consequences. Boris valued the situation and perceived as much more dangerous the power that could give the communist party in his country so strongly supported by Moscow (and by the Bulgarian people markedly Russophile), that the advantages that Germany offered them (for which the highest Bulgarian hierarchies bet). And the decision was very fast, since the war arrived in Greece after the Italian attack and Germany requested to be able to operate from Bulgarian territory to support the Italians. Initially, Bulgarian King Boris III allowed German military personnel to organize preparations for German intervention on Bulgarian territory, but in the end he had to position himself and adher to the "Tripartite Pact" on 1 March 1941.

By joining the Axis, King Boris hoped that Yugoslavia would follow the same path, despite Macedonia being cut off in favor of the Bulgarians. But the situation changed drastically when the Yugoslav government was overthrown by a popular revolt. But now with Bulgaria on its side, Germany would have a good launching base for its ground and air troops along the borders Bulgaria had with Yugoslavia and Greece in a blitz that will begin on APRIL 6, 1941. At the end of that month, the 2nd and 5th Bulgarian Armies had already occupied their territories assigned by Germany, in Yugoslavia and Greece.

The participation of Bulgaria in this operation consisted mainly in acting as an operational base for the German armies. And thanks to this aid and without having to fire a shot, Bulgaria was rewarded with the occupation of territories in the south and southeast of Yugoslavia and in the northeast of Greece, which historically had corresponded with Thrace and Macedonia (well-known as Belomorie to the Bulgarians). Although this gift for services rendered was poisoned since in both the Yugoslav and Greek occupied territories there would be a widespread rejection of the alleged process of Bulgarization which was ordered in the new territories (which consisted of settling Bulgarian settlers in recently acquired lands, added to the massive deportations of those they resisted it or the elimination of the rebels). This initial rejection turned into a genuine guerrilla war that kept the Bulgarian army in action until 1944, when a new turn of events would occur in the country's history, which we will comment shortly. The executions carried out by the Bulgarians alone in their Greek territories reached 15,000 dead, so that the direction of the exodus of many of the Thracians went to the Greek lands occupied by the Germans, less violent than that of the Bulgarian zone.

What had motivated the fact that in a few years the traditionally Russophile Bulgaria (due to its common Slavic origin) would have ended up in league with the German Reich, was the desire not to confront a powerful Germany and the multiple benefits that they would get with low cost. In fact, this Bulgarian political duality led to the fact that, even after the participation in the Axis on June 22, 1941 (date of the beginning of the "Barbarossa Operation" or the German invasion of the USSR) Bulgaria was invited to fight against the Soviets but refused the possibility of confronting their Russian "Slav brothers", thus being reduced initially to their activity to dominate their new territories in Yugoslavia and Greece. Despite this, some skirmishes carried out against the Russians by the Bulgarian Navy and Air Force in areas where they materially coincided with the Soviets were inevitable, as was the case of the fleet that the Soviets held in the Black Sea attacking Axis ships.

But the Reich demanded more from Bulgaria, and following the attack on Pearl Harbor in December 1941 and the subsequent entry of United States into the War, the Bulgarian government had to declare war on the Western Allies. King Boris III again found himself in such a critical situation that he even considered suicide or abdication. Although in a way, having no frontier with enemy countries, this declaration of war was essentially nominal. But as the war progressed and when the Reich began to decline, the Allies retook the initiative, drastically changing the situation. Thus, in August 1943, Bulgaria would awaken from that dream of inner peace with the presence of hundreds of American aircraft in their airspace. Initially the targets of these bombers were located in the Romanian oil areas, although new targets were added immediately in Bulgaria, where Sofia would be a frequent target. During this period between 1943 and 1944 is when most of the interventions of the Bulgarian air force in the conflict took place, although we will have the opportunity to discover that they were not even the only ones.

In August 1943 another very important event occurred in Bulgaria since king Boris III suddenly died on the 28th, leaving his position to his son Simeon II (still a minor). Thus, the Bulgarian people passed from a unifying king of his people that had been able to ride out these hard first years of war to a king that could not govern having to hand his government to three regents.

The situation in which Bulgaria was left after the intense bombings, the death of the king and the situation of Germany in 1944 led Prime Minister Dobri Bozhilov to start talks with a view to changing sides in the world conflict; which as we will see below finally paid off, although perhaps not the way desired by the Bulgarians themselves, since they would remain under the Soviet "fold" after the end of the war.

As we commented, 1944 was a year in which the Bulgarian people would again give a new twist on its history. On September 2, the Russian Army was approaching with great speed towards Bulgaria, so that is the reason why the possibility of having to face their Russian "brothers" while they supported a declining Germany (that at the end of August was in full retreat towards the Reich). That situation led to a political movement that on the same day (September 2) led to the creation of a new Bulgarian government that quickly made peace with the Allies, expelled the Germans from their territory and declared themselves neutral. But the Soviets were not going to let the Bulgarians escape so easily after being united to the Axis, the reason why it declared war on it on 5 September and began to reach into Bulgarian territory, where it did not meet resistance. The situation was clear, everything was lost and the Red Army was entering Bulgaria, so another change in direction was happening. And this consisted of a veritable coup d'état that took place on September 9, establishing a pro-Soviet government in power.

Once the change of side of Bulgaria in the World War II was carried out, for the first time in the conflict, the Bulgarian troops would be called to fight at the front, although in this case against their old German ally.

The Bulgarian Army was incorporated into the 3rd Ukrainian Front of the Soviet Army, now fighting in Yugoslavia and Hungary. To demonstrate its "loyalty" to its new ally, it had to fight hard against the Germans, that caused them numerous casualties. For its part, the BAF had to fly hundreds of missions between September and November 1944 supporting the Soviet forces in their advance from the south towards the Reich. The fight ended in the north with the liberation of northern Serbia on December 2, beginning the process of sovietizing Bulgaria. As a clear example of this, in JANUARY 1945 new equipment of Soviet origin comes to substitute in part (and definitely in the future) the equipment of mainly German origin that the Bulgarians had.

But Bulgaria did not change sides at the last minute and became a winner in the conflict because the inevitable happened: the territories annexed in Greece and Yugoslavia had to be returned and therefore repatriate about 150,000 individuals of Bulgarian origin settled in these lands; in addition to other conditions that also had to be fulfilled like the delivery of war material, etc. On the contrary, the Bulgarians were allowed to continue control of Dobrudja at the expense of Romania's possible interests in those lands.

CHAPTER II

History of the Bulgarian Air Force (BAF)

Although clearly the BAF began its existence before, in our text we are going to only deal with the period that really has to do with the BAF as it appeared in the second world conflict; bearing always in mind the superb works of Nedialkov and Neulen.

1920–1930

The Air Force that Bulgaria possessed during World War II was the result of many diplomatic activities led mainly by King Boris III in order to be able to live up to the demands of the new world order after the war (we remember that after World War I and Signature in 1919 of the "Treaty of Paris", the Bulgarian air forces were practically eliminated).

After that Treaty, the air fleet declined to practically non-operational levels, but as in Germany, some aircraft were used sneakily for the training and practices of future combat pilots. Already in 1921 the "Section of the Aeronautical Gendarmerie" under the control of the Ministry of War concealed such "illegal" training, and although France succeeded in eliminating it with its political pressure, it soon revived again with the name of the Aeronautical Section of the Ministry of Railways, Posts and Telegraphs. In 1923 the first pilot-cadets began their training at the Vrazhdebna Flight School, located in Sofia; in 1924 the Aeronautical Section grew to become the Aeronautical Directory still under the control of the same ministry.

It was obvious that more aircraft were needed and also ones more suitable for the training of new pilots, and the best way to provide them was domestic production which could allow the future self-sufficiency in aircraft for Bulgaria.

In 1924 the government of Bulgaria acquired 18 aircraft abroad, of which 16 were French and 2 British. Thanks to these aircraft a new cycle began in the history of military aviation in Bulgaria.

In 1925 the State´s Aeronautical Construction Workshops were created usually known as DAR, in Bozhurishte. Aircraft of the WWI era were built there like the "Uzounov-1" or DAR-U1 (Bulgarian variant of the German DFW CV) and the DAR-

2 (another Bulgarian variant of a German aircraft, in this case the Albatros C. III); although national designs like the DAR-1 were also produced. During the same year, 17 new aircraft were acquired, including 2 Italian seaplanes.

1930–1938

But it is in the 30's when the core of what became the Royal Bulgarian Air Force (Bulgarski Voennovazdushni Sili – BVVS) was formed, which we will generally call the Bulgarian Air Force (BAF), since in 1930 it was controlled by the military that used an Aeronautical Regiment that included those air units which in a clandestine manner were used in several operations. Despite its creation as an entity, the BAF remained subordinate to the Army.

Continuing with its slow growth, Bulgarian aeronautics will take a new step, since in 1931 the Italian aircraft industry Caproni established an aircraft factory in Kasanlak leading to the creation of Caproni-Bulgara (Bulgarski Caproni or Kaproni-Bulgarska). Actually this aeronautical factory began its days as a Bulgarian branch of the Czechoslovak company Aero, but in the early 30's Caproni built the factory, under the condition of using it for at least 10 years.

That same year, engineer Lazarov completed the design of a two-seater training plane, the DAR-6, from which five years later the more evolved DAR-6 will emerge.

In 1932 the Aeronautical Regiment becomes the Aerial Force or BAF (in Bulgarian to be called Air Regiment) and will have to wait until July 28, 1934 before the BAF is reestablished officially and the Aeronautical Regiment became the Air Force or BAF (in the Bulgarian language: Vazdushni Voyski or VV), which according to Nedialkov and Neulen was structured with a Headquarters, two Army Air Groups (based at the aerodromes of Plovdiv and Bozhurishte), a Training Group (also based in Plovdiv), a Maritime Squadron (Chaika base in the vicinity of Varna) and other small support units.

In 1935 the Bozhurishte aerodrome was assigned the first Air Force Group composed of four squadrons (one fighter, two reconnaissance and one training).

Once the step to formalize the new air force was done, the next development was to give strength to it, so that numerous efforts were made dedicated to increasing the number of aircraft and therefore air units. In 1936 commercial relations between Germany and Bulgaria were increasing with the arrival of aircraft that began to become obsolete in the Reich (although they were considered as first line in Bulgaria) like the He.45 "Schturkel", He.51 "Sokol", He .72, FW-44 or Fw-56, of which about 42 examples were obtained. In 1937, the arrival of two multi-purpose aircraft, Fw.58 "Gulub" (pigeon), and a number of bombers such as the Do.11D "Prilep", which were obsolete for the Germans but in Bulgaria were considered as first line until the arrival of modern equipment.

It was in June 1937 when Bulgaria was finally released from the draconian conditions that it had been subjected since WW I, which allowed the establishment of an Air Force that now, would began to grow and be restructured in a fully operational manner.

King Boris III was one of the great architects of Bulgarian aviation development during these years, and without delay he began to seek new aircraft for the Bulgarian Air Force in the flourishing European aeronautic market. It was in 1937 during the military parade on the day of the patron of the Bulgarian Armed Forces, St. George, when the Air Force first appeared as a part of the Armed Forces. And it took only a few more days, on June 27, 1937, at the Bozhurishte airfield where the "official presentation" took place to the world of the BAF where the new aerial regiments were shown as well as their brand new combat flags. There King Boris III reviewed 12 brand new Ar.65 "Orel" fighters and 12 Do.11D bombers, which had been paid for by the monarch's own money (such was his involvement in this enterprise).

Only a year later the Bulgarian government obtained a French bank credit for 375 million francs to obtain weapons and buy materials for the improvement of roads and railways.

Also in 1938, the air fleet grew again, in this case because of the acquisition of new German aircraft also thanks to the intervention of Boris III, specifically 12 He.51 fighters and 12 He.45 reconnaissance aircraft. In 1938 the feverish search for aircraft with which to complete the nascent air force continued, and on this occasion Poland was the supplier country. From there were acquired 14 brand new PZL.24B "Yastreb" fighters along with 12 PZL.43B "Chaika" light-attack bombers that were beginning to increase the abilities and potential of the BAF. A second batch of 20 PZL.24 C acquired by Bulgaria to Poland is spoken of, but in several sources this acquisition is not confirmed, although Bulgarian interest in them is recorded. Other aircraft were received from German surpluses such as two Ju.523m "Sova", four Fw.58 multipurpose aircraft, six He.72 "Karnache", six Fw-44 "Vrabche" and six Fw-56 "Komar".

On the other hand, the national industry increased the aircraft park, since it contributed to the BAF 12 DAR-3 "Garvan-3", 28 KB-4 "Chuchuliga-2" (Skylark-2) and 45 KB-5 "Chuchuliga-3 ". Other aircraft of national origin were KB-1 "Peperuda" (butterfly), KB-2UT, KB-2A "Chuchuliga" or KB-3 "Chuchuliga-1". Although all these planes would not be first line combat material, they were very useful in other diverse roles.

After the agreement of Thessalonica of 1938, the hell that had resulted from the Treaty of Neully, imposed by the winning powers in the First World War, was over. Matters about air defense were immediately planned, so the antiaircraft artillery was strengthened and 140 of the best young pilots from the Flight Schools were sent to receive advanced training courses in Germany, first at the School of Gliders in Kaufbeuren and later at the Flight School at Werneuchen. These included practices with modern models of Bf.109 D and E, but were mainly training on other aircraft such as Bücker 181, Arado Ar 45, Arado Ar 68, Heinkel He.51 and Focke Wulf Fw 56. Further on when the G model of the Bf.109 was available, pilots could also be sent to carry out advanced training in them.

Most of the time, these new pilots, when returning, were attached to their new combat units, in other cases (such as the future Bulgarian ace Stoyan Stoyanov) will be sent to the Bulgarian flying schools as instructors and in other cases they completed their training in combat zones attached to German units (although not combat). This last case would happen to the well-known pilot Dimitar Spissarevski who in the summer of 1943 was sent to the English Channel next to another pilot to familiarise himself in combat tactics with his companions in the Luftwaffe.

It was in June 1938 when the first seven Bulgarian pilots went to Germany for their training in various aspects of flying and combat; and among them was the afore mentioned Stoyanov. A second group composed of five new pilots travelled to Germany in March of 1939 and in that one was the afore mentioned Spisarevski. The majority of the pilots sent to Germany in the different batches would return to Bulgaria no later than 1940.

Italy, although markedly less important than Germany, also collaborated in the training of new Bulgarian pilots, so that in 1940 twenty Bulgarian pilots completed their training at the Military Aeronautical Academy in Caserta. There are also reports of some Bulgarian pilots who received flying training in allied Hungary.

Finally, and also related to the training of new pilots, I should mention that not only fighter pilots had the opportunity to train in Germany, but also attack pilots. Thus in the second half of 1941, 15 attack pilots were selected to train at Stuka-Vorschule 3 in Bad Aibling and Stuka-Vorschule 1 in Wertheim, where they were able to catch up with their German comrades dedicated to the dive bombing attacks. These pilots after completing their training course were sent to Italy to gain operational experience, but the BAF rejected the possibility that their pilots could act in the Mediterranean against Allied ships. These men would be the nucleus of the formation of the future 2nd Attack Regiment or Shturmovy.

Simultaneously with the acquisition of new aircraft for the BAF, it was of great importance to get new pilots to serve on those machines. This was achieved thanks to the Orlyak Training (Yunker) in Vrazhdebna Military School and the Kazanluk Air School. These were complemented by the Dolna Mitropolia Fighter School (which later moved to Karlovo) and Telish's "Blind" Flight School. By the end of 1938, no less than 184 pilots and 89 observers had been instructed, along with a few other specialists who would form the core of the different air units that would bring Bulgaria into the world conflict.

The structure of BAF in June 1937 was as follows (according Mr. Nedialkov, Aeroflight.co.uk and Mr. Neulen sources):

Headquarters of the Vazdushni Voyski (VV or Air Force) based in Sofia.
1st Army Orlyak (based in Bozhuriste):
– Fighter Yato: with 12 He.51.
– Reconnaissance Yato: with 12 He.45.
– Training Yato: with 6 DAR-3.
2nd Army Orlyak (based in Plovdiv):
– Bomber Yato: with 12 Do.11.
3rd Army Orlyak (based in Bozhuriste):
– Training Yato: with 12 Ar.65 and 6 KB-2A.
Training Orlyak (based in Kazanluk):
– Airplane School: with 8 DAR-1A, 9 KB-1 and 8 KB-2UT.

1939

But the political activity in Europe would benefit in a certain way the acquisition of new aircraft, since after the occupation of Czechoslovakia with the formation of the Protectorate of Bohemia and Moravia, the Air Force of that country ceased to exist. Their remains were used by the Germans to supply planes somewhat more advanced than those they offered to their allies. So according to Nedialkov and Neulen, Bulgaria took the opportunity and bought for a symbolic price 78 biplane fighters B.534, 32 B-71 bombers (a Czech licensed version of Soviet light bomber SB also known in Spain as Katiuskas), 60 S-328 reconnaissance biplanes and 12 Aero MB 200 bombers (a licensed version of French Bloch 200) that were to be used for training, 28 training Avia Bs-122 and some B-304. They also reached an agreement with Avia to supply B.534 and B-135 in the summer of 1939. This maneuver was very favorable for both sides, German and Bulgarian, as the former supplied arms to their allies and the latter paid for such aircraft with a 60% discount of its original price and the possibility of paying in kind (tobacco and other Bulgarian production goods). Indeed, negotiations with Czechoslovakia for the acquisition of aircraft of Czech origin had begun at least a month before the occupation by Germany; in spite of this, the Bulgarians asserted their rights of acquisition of the aircraft in front of their new Germanic owners.

Another important step was motivated by the good impression made by the acquired Polish aircraft, so that according to Glass at the end of 1938 – early 1939 a new batch of 42 PZL-43B and 8 PZL-24F were requested (similar to the B model, although with a new engine that offered better performance). This request could be fulfilled by Poland since the German invasion that took place on September 1, 1939 had not yet occurred, although four of the PZL.24F were destroyed in the German bombing of Poland (at the Okecie factory in September, 1939) and two of the PZL.43 had to be delivered by the German government after the German conquest of Poland as late as 1941.

To all this material of foreign origin, an abundant local production has to be added thanks to the two emerging aeronautical industries of the country, the DAR and the CB. This national production allowed Bulgaria to get suitable aircraft mainly for training tasks, but without ruling out a role as reconnaissance and even attack.

In only three years, the BAF stocks had increased dramatically, rising to having 478 aircraft of which about 135 were of Bulgarian production.

The general provision of the BAF in 1939 prior to the WWII was based on the Air Regiments (Orlyak) for fighter, bombing, reconnaissance and basic training. Each Orlyak was organised by squadrons (Yatos) of one type or another according to each Orlyak. Despite the following provision of the structure of the BAF (based on that of the expert on the subject, Dimitar Nedialkov) is admittedly a somewhat confusing issue because of the number of variations that structuring suffered from the years prior to war until the end of it.

To be clearer about the number of aircraft in each unit, use this approximate table (based on Mr. Neulen work):

Name	No. of aircraft	Designation
Polk	120	Wing
Orlyak	40	Group
Yato	12–15	Squadron
Krilo	4	Flight
Dvoika	2	Couple

Another thing to keep in mind is how to represent the belonging to an Orlyak of a Polk, which for example would be: 3/6 corresponds to 3rd Orlyak of the 6th Polk.

It should also be considered that, at the outset of hostilities, the entire organizational structure and structure of the BAF (as Nedialkov reports) was implemented in men and machines. So that of 4,240 men (of which there were 342 officers) and 374 aircraft (211 combat and 163 training) during the peacetime period, 19,451 men (with 1,163 officers) and 495 aircraft (of which they were 213 combat) that were distributed in an Air Eskadra with three Polk (Fighter, bombing and from Army) that totaled 162 aircraft; and a Support Air Polk with 51 aircraft (distributed in three reconnaissance Yatos and one long range reconnaissance unit).

The provision at the outset of hostilities in Europe, not in Bulgaria, was as follows (according Mr. Nedialkov, Aeroflight.co.uk and Mr. Neulen sources):

1st Line Orlyak (Army support): based in Bozhurishte and commanded by Major Vulkov. With three frontline Yato and another training. Made up of 36 PZL.43 reconnaissance and light attack, as well as 11 training aircraft. Being divided into:

- 113 Yato: with 12 PZL.43.
- 123 Yato: with 12 PZL.43.

– 133 Yato: with 12 PZL.43.

– 142 Training Yato: with 3 DAR-3 and 6 KB-4.

2nd Fighter Orlyak (istrebitelen = fighter): based in Karlovo and commanded by major Georgiev. Conformed by four Fighter Yatos (with 12–15 B.534 by Yato) with 71 B.534 and 12 training aircraft and advanced training. Under the command of this Orlyak was the Fighter School that counted 33 training aircraft of several types (based in Dolna Metropolia). Being divided into:

– 212 Yato: with 15 B.534.

– 222 Yato: with 15 B.534.

– 232 Yato: with 15 B.534.

– 242 Yato: with 15 B.534.

– 253 Training Yato: with 10–12 B-122 and 11 B.534.

– Fighter School: with 19 B-122, 12 Ar.65, 12 He.51, 6 Bü-131 and 6 Fw-56.

3rd Reconnaissance Orlyak (razuznavatelen = recognition): based in Yambol and commanded by Major Karadimchev. Formed by four reconnaisance Yatos and one training Yato. Featuring 48 S-328 (12 for Yato) and 12 various training aircraft. Being divided into:

– 313 Yato: with 12 S-328.

– 323 Yato: with 12 S-328.

– 333 Yato: with 12 S-328.

– 343 Yato: with 12 S-328.

– 373 Training yato: with 3 DAR-3 and 6 KB-4.

5th Bomber Orlyak (bombardirovicen = bombing): based in Plovdiv and commanded by Major Stoykov. It had three Bomber Yato and a training one. The planes they had were 12 Do.11 (which formed a Yato) and 24 B-71 (with 12 for Yato), in addition to 15 training aircraft. Also under the shelter of this Orlyak was the School of "Blind" Flight (instrumental) with 18 training aircraft adapted to this function and based in Telish. Being divided into:

– 515 Yato: with 12 B-72.

– 525 Yato: with 12 B-72.

– 535 Yato: with 12 Do.11.

– 545 Training yato: with 12 MB-200.

– School of "Blind" Flight (instrumental): with Fw.58 and Ju.52.

Training Units:

Orlyak of Training Yunker (instruktorskiego = training): based on the aerodrome at Vrazhdebna in Sofia and under the command of Major Dimitrov. With three training Yatos and 62 training aircraft of several types. Being divided into:

– 1st Yato: with 20 Fw-44.

– 2nd Yato: with 20 Fw-44.

– 3rd Yato: with He.72, KB-3, KB-4 and Fw-56.

Air School: based in Kazanluk and under the command of Major Drenikov. With three training Yatos and 52 varied training aircraft. Being divided into:
   – 1st Training Yato: with DAR-1A, DAR-6, Bü-131 and Fw-44.
   – 2nd Training Yato: with DAR-8, KB-2A and KB-4.
   – 3rd Training Yato: with KB-5 and DAR-3.

Training Orlyak: based at Vrazhdebna aerodrome in Sofia. With one Training Yato and one Fighter Yato. It had 11 PZL.24, nine PZL.43, and 11 He.45. Being divided into:
   – Line Yato: with 9 PZL.43.
   – Fighter Yato: with 11 PZL.24.
   – Reconnaissance Yato: with 11 He.45.

1940

At the beginning of WWII, again the BAF increased its air arsenal, in this case with material from the Reich. In this way 10 Messerschmitt Bf.109E-4 fighters, 11 Dornier Do.17M (bombers) and P (reconnaissance), 6 Messerschmitt Bf.108 dedicated to liaison, 24 Arado Ar.96B-2 for advanced training and 14 Bücker -Bestmann Bü-131 also trainers, were acquired.

The arrival of the Bf.109 requires a special mention due to the importance of their presence at the BAF. In early March 1940 a Bulgarian delegation reached an agreement with the Germans to be supplied 10 Bf.109E3, which was entered into a contract signed on 4 APRIL . The aircraft acquired were obviously not the most modern that Germany had at the time, but still another small "issue" has to be added as a simplified model was purchased. This meant (according to Nedialkov) that the aircraft had no oxygen system (so they could not be used at levels over 5000 meters) and that they were armed with two MG 17 7.92 mm machine guns but they did not have the two MG FF 20 mm guns. Although finally these two issues were corrected since the cannons were paid for separately and later an oxygen system for the aircraft was acquired in the spring of 1941, as well as several spare parts.

The ten purchased Bf.109E3 were transported by rail from the factory in Wiener Neustadt to Bulgaria, where they arrived in June. As the planes were dismantled, the task of assembling and tuning them had to be started, which was carried out in some installations located next to the aerodrome of Bozhurishte and always with the collaboration of German advisors.

Once assembled and tuned up, they had to be flight tested by the German test pilot Wacker and sent to the Marno Pole airfield in the vicinity of the city of Karlovo. At first there were 20 Bulgarian pilots who would receive training to fly the German fighter, although in later years with the arrival of new planes of more advanced models, this number would grow.

Not only was Bulgaria buying abroad, but internal production continued, and in 1940 national industries supplied the BAF with 42 DAR-9, 45 KB-5 and the first twin-engine KB-6. By the end of 1940, the BAF owned over 600 aircraft, of which 258 were combat aircraft; and 10,287 men served in its ranks. Although to be realistic, these figures can be misleading, since their only moderately modern aircraft in conditions of parity with other European air forces were the Bf.109 and although somewhat obsolete, the Do.17. The rest of the fighter planes consisted of the outclassed PZL.24 or B.534 biplanes; while in the bombers area, the B-71s were outdated but the Do.11 and the MB 200 were completely obsolete when it came to fighting against any air force participating in the current European conflict.

In spite of this situation, let's take into account that in just over four years, the BAF was reborn from its ashes like a phoenix and spread its wings over the Bulgarian map, which was not easy after more than 20 years condemned to be not able to grow; in fact from May 30 the BAF is considered as a Force independent of the other military branches of the Kingdom of Bulgaria. Other important aspects of air defense, such as aerial surveillance and antiaircraft artillery, were also carefully studied. Since June 1940 a network of air observers was been deployed across the country to monitor any type of enemy air movement over Bulgaria. According to Nedialkov, Bulgaria would have four Warning Centers specially dedicated to control the southeast region. They did not have sophisticated equipment and were based solely on visual observation, although gradually they will have radio equipment to form 34 radio stations throughout the country. As far as the artillery was concerned, it was based only on guns of 88 mm and 62 mm. As a great advantage for this still underdeveloped antiaircraft defense, the 12th German Army offered support in this regard with its own antiaircraft defenses and later even with Freya radars around the country.

During this year, a new and ambitious plan in the BAF will fail. We are referring to the construction program in Bulgaria of the Czech Avia B-135 aircraft, an aircraft that the Government of Bulgaria had been interested in since 1939. As stated above, Bulgaria held firm to its rights to build them by means of a license for the B-135 fighter, as agreed with the Avia before the German occupation of Czechoslovakia. The contract with Avia consisted of the acquisition within two years of 12 examples of the B-135 (which was no more than an improved model of the B-35 fighter) built by the Avia, and the license production of 50 new planes at the DAR facilities with the obligation to use engines, weapons and flight instruments supplied by the Czechs. Of the 12 + 50 planes planned, only the first 12 were delivered to the BAF by the DAR in Lovech in the summer of 1943. The official name for the B-135 aircraft manufactured in Bulgaria was to be DAR-11 "Lyastovitsa" (Swallow), but the first 12 were always called Avia B-135. The difficulty of DAR to build this aircraft, the delay in the realization of the program (the B-135 was only an average plane in 1940, but in 1942 it was completely outdated) and the small number of manufactured units determined their fate: the newly manufactured aircraft did not go to fighter units but to those of advanced training. In spite of this, they would still have a "day of glory" on March 30, 1944, a fact that will be discussed a little later.

As an important fact regarding the structure of the BAF, this year there was another new restructuring that aimed to increase the effectiveness of the same in which the basis of the air units will be the Polk. On 1 July 1940 the structure was as follows (according Mr. Nedialkov, Aeroflight.co.uk and Mr. Neulen sources):

Headquarters of VV based in Sofia.

1st Army Polk (based in Karlovo):
- 1st Reconnaissance: with 12 S-328.
- 2nd Reconnaissance: with 12 S-328.
- 1st Army Yato: with 12 PZL.43.
- 1st Fighter Yato: with 15 B.534.

2nd Army Polk
- 1st Reconnaissance Yato: with 12 S-328.
- 2nd Reconnaissance Yato: with 12 S-328.
- 1st Army Yato: with 12 PZL.43.
- 1st Fighter Yato: with 15 B.534.

3rd Army Polk (based on Yambol):
- 1st Reconnaissance Yato: with 12 S-328.
- 2nd Reconnaissance Yato: with 12 S-328.
- 1st Army Yato: with 12 PZL.43.
- 1st Fighter Yato: with 15 B.534.

4th Army Polk
- 1st Reconnaissance Yato: with 12 S-328.
- 2nd Reconnaissance Yato: with 12 S-328.
- 1st Army Yato: with 12 PZL.43.
- 1st Fighter Yato: with 15 B.534.

5th Bomber Polk (based in Plovdiv):
- 1st Bomber Orlyak:
515 th Yato: with 12 B-71.
525th Yato: with 12 B-71.
- 2nd Bomber Orlyak:
535th Yato: with 12 B-71.
Unknown number Yato:?
545th Training Yato: with 12 MB-200.

6th Fighter Polk (based in Karlovo):
- 1st Fighter Orlyak:
1st Yato: with 15 B.534.

2nd Yato: with 15 B.534.
– 2nd Fighter Orlyak:
3rd Yato: with 15 B.534.
253th Training Yato: with 10 B.534 and 10 B-122.
Acrobatic school: with 19 B-122, 12 Ar.65, 12 He.51, 6 Fw-56 and 6 Bü-131.

Training Units:
Orlyak Officers Training (based in Vrazhdebna):
– 1st Yato: with 20 Fw-44.
– 2nd Yato: with 20 Fw-44.
– 3rd Yato: with Fw-56, KB-3, KB-4 and He.72.
Training Polk (with Kazanluk as main base):
– 1st Training Orlyak (Air School):
1st Training Yato: with DAR-9.
2nd Training Yato: unknown type of plane.
3rd Training Yato: unknown type of plane
– 2nd Training Orlyak:
School of "Blind" Flight (instrumental): (based in Telish): with Ju.52 and Fw.58.
– 3rd Training Orlyak (based in Stara Goza):
1st Army Yato: unknown type of plane.
2nd Attack Yato: with PZL.43.
3rd Fighter Yato: unknown type of plane.

Technical School of NCOs (based in Kazanluk).
As it can be seen, great importance was given to the training aspect of new pilots and not only in Bulgarian lands, since a number of men would also be sent to be trained in Germany, Italy or Hungary.

1941

This year marked the development of Bulgaria during WWII, since after joining the "Tripartite Pact" on March 1, 1941, it began its dangerous journey. Only one day after its signature, the German 12th Army and Fliegerkorps VIII began their deployment in inner Bulgaria. As regards the BAF, the Luftwaffe instructors and other specialists who had entered the country were attached to the various Bulgarian squadrons. After "Operation Marita" began on 6 APRIL , Bulgaria did not participate in the attack but did reinforce its defensive measures against possible attacks from Greece and Yugoslavia. But they did not have to wait, because several attacks from Yugoslav and RAF aircraft were launched against Bulgaria. In particular, as Nedialkov, Neulen and Boshniakov, refer, the first attack was by 4 Yugoslav Do.17Kb-1 that attacked the city of Kustendil and its railway station (west of Sofia and about 20 km from the border with Yugoslavia) on 6 APRIL , causing the death of 47 people and injuries to another 95, most of them, as expected, civilians. This attack meant that aircraft of the 2nd Orlyak (B.534) were sent urgently to Bozhuriste.

To this initial attack followed other limited bombing of the aerodromes of Petrich, Varba and Ichtiman, where units of the Luftwaffe had their bases. Other small Bulgarian towns and even the railway station at Sofia received the brave but weak Yugoslav response. Also from Greece, Wellington bombers of the RAF managed to hit Bulgarian territory, although as in the Yugoslav case, with little effect although leaving the "message" that could reach any area of the country due to the minimal capacity of response of its air defense units. The only possibility was that the anti-aircraft defenses could intimidate the Yugoslavs or British, because despite attempts to intercept the enemy bombers, the B.534s were completely useless in this regard.

The disposition of the BAF before the "Marita Operation", led different units to change their location in the direction of the borders as we have seen. The 13 units that were affected by it, were the recently created 1/1, 1/6 and 2/6 Orlyak and a fighter Yato. These units were composed of:

1/1 composed by three Yatos of B.534 with 34 aircraft in total based in Bozhuriste.

1/6 composed by two Yatos with 10 Bf.109E3 and 11 PZL.24B based in Asen

2/6 composed by two B.534 Yatos with 12 aircraft each, based in Dabene.

Fighter Yato: 12 B.534 based in Okop.

On the other hand according to Nedialkov, it also updated the anti-aircraft defense provision of some areas of the country, basically the strategic areas of Sofia and Bozhuriste. In Sofia an Anti-aircraft Artillery Unit was deployed consisting of two Heavy Batteries (with 8 x 88mm anti-aircraft guns), two Light Artillery Companies (with 6 x 20mm anti-aircraft guns) and a Projector Company (with three 1500mm). Evidently, the Early Warning Service was strengthened, with four Alert Centers (all in the southeast region, where the arrival of the enemy was expected), eight Alert Posts (with shortwave radio stations) and 34 Radio Stations (provided with VHF radios); being all controlled and coordinated from the transmitter located on Mount Vitosha.

During this year, the arrival of the new aircraft material was reduced compared to previous years. So that only 9 fighters Bf.109E7, two PZL.43B ground attack, 3 Fi.156 liaison, two Ju.523m transport, two He.42 seaplanes (and possibly some He.60 also) and 15 Do.17Kb1 ex-Yugoslavs bombers obtained as trophies of war, were acquired by the BAF.

The BAF in 1941 with 561 machines (of which 411 were operational) had an approximate inventory as follows (based on Neulen and Volkov):

Fighter Number

Bf.109E – 18

B.534 – 73

PZL.24 – 11

Bombers

Do.17 – 18

B-71 – 32

B-200 – 12 (used as trainers)

Light attack and bombers

PZL.43 – 33

DAR-10 – 1

Reconnaissance and light attack

S-328 – 60

KB-5III – 42

DAR-3 – 22

He.45 – 10

Advanced training

B-122 – 29

Ar.65 – 11

Fw.56 – 4

He.51 – 1

Training

Fw.44 – 39

K3 – 25

Ar.96 – 24

KB-3 – 19

He.45 – 11

Bü.133 – 10

DAR-8 – 6

DAR_9 – 6

He.72 – 5

Liaison

KB-6 – 9

Fw.58 – 8

Bf.108 – 6

Fi.156 – 3

Seaplanes

He.42 – 2

He.60 – 2

Transport

Do.11 – 12 (also liaison)

Ju.523m – 2

The Black Sea became a strategic region for Bulgaria even more important than it has been before the conflict. For its control, a unit called a mixed Yato, that grouped two Krilos, was "created": one located in the aerodrome of Balchik (belonging to the 2nd Army Polk and equipped with 5 S-328) and the other one was located in the aerodrome of Safarovo (belonging to the 3rd Polk of the Army and equipped with 4 S-328). For this task a transfer of two Yatos belonging to the 5th Bombardment Polk (one with 9 Do.17M and one with 6 B-71) from Plovdiv to the Kavalla airfield was required. Thanks to these new planes, better prepared and less obsolete than the S-328s, the BAF managed to operate patrol flights as far as the island of Crete, with S-328 being reserved for shorter flights.

At this time it is advisable to remember the seaplanes of German origin which the BAF was equipped with. Bulgaria's intention was to acquire modern and capable marine reconnaissance Ar.196A3 aircraft to effectively monitor the Bulgarian waters of the Black Sea and serve as a deterrent against the Soviet vessels that swarmed there. Due to the German inability at that time to supply such aircraft (which will at last happen in 1943), two Heinkel He.42 seaplanes were supplied to the Bulgarians for the purpose of using them as crew trainers who would operate the longed-for Ar.196A3 in the future. In that same negotiation, Germany yielded two He.60D seaplanes (also obsolete like He.42, although highly desired by Bulgaria as they would be the spearhead of its maritime reconnaissance). The He.60Ds were integrated into the 161st Squadron of Maritime Cooperation based in Peinerdiyk, near Varna. In this way, surveillance tasks were started not only on the coast, but also in depth in the Black Sea waters that Bulgaria controlled; although as we have said, it will not be until 1943 with the arrival of the seaplanes Arado when this Unit would be operational.

The main air bases (Air Baza) from which the aircraft of the BAF operated were those of Bozhuriste, Gorna Oryahovica and Stara Zagora. The arrival of new aircraft of German and Yugoslav origin, resulted in several modifications to the structural composition of the BAF, being on the first of August 1941 as follows (according Mr. Nedialkov, Aeroflight.co.uk and Mr. Neulen sources):

Headquarters of VV based in Sofia.

Units deployed on the front line:

– Mixed Yato:

1st Krilo (formerly belonging to the 2nd Army Polk): with 5 S-328 based Balchik.

2nd Krilo (formerly belonging to the 3rd Army Polk): with 4 S-328 based on Safarovo.

1st Army Polk (based in Karlovo):

– 1st Reconnaissance Yato: with 12 S-328.

– 2nd Reconnaissance Yato: with 12 S-328.

– 1st Army Yato: with 12 PZL.43.

– 1 Fighter Orlyak (composed by three Yatos):

1st Fighter Yato: with 11 B.534.

2nd Fighter Yato: : with 11 B.534.

3rd Fighter Yato: with 12 B.534.

2nd Army Polk

– 1st Reconnaissance Yato: with 12 S-328.

– 2nd Reconnaissance Yato: with 12 S-328.

– 1st Army Yato: with 12 PZL.43.

– 1st Fighter Yato: with 15 B.534.

3rd Army Polk

– 1st Reconnaissance Yato: with 12 S-328. Based in Yambol.

– 2nd Reconnaissance Yato: with 12 S-328. Based in Yambol.

– 333rd Army Yato: with 6 S-328. Based in Sarafovo.

– 1st Fighter Yato with 12 B.534. Possibly based in Okop.

4th Army Polk:

– 1st Reconnaissance Yato with 12 S-328.

– 2nd Reconnaissance Yato: with 12 S-328.

– 443rd Army Yato: with 9 S-328. Based in Kavala.

– 1st Fighter Yato:: with 15 B.534.

5th Bomber Polk:

– 1st Bomber Orlyak:

Yato?: with 9 Do.17. Based in Kavala.

Yato?: with Do.17Kb1 and Do.17M. Based in Plovdiv.

– 2nd Bomber Orlyak:

Yato?: with 12 B-71. Based in Plovdiv.

Yato?: with 6 B-71. Based in Kavala.

545 Training Yato: with 12 MB-200. Based in Plovdiv.

6th Fighter Polk (based on Karlovo):

– 1st Fighter Orlyak:

1st Yato: with 10 Bf.109E4. Based in Asen.

2nd Yato: with 11 PZL.24. Based in Asen.

– 2nd Fighter Orlyak:

3rd Yato: with 12 B.534. Based in Dabene.

4th Yato: with 12 B.534. Based in Dabene.

Transport Yato.

Liaison Yato (Yato Kurierskiego).

Training Units:

Orlyak Officers Training, based in Vrazhdebna and composed of:

– 1st Yato: with 20 Fw-44.

– 2nd Yato: with 20 Fw-44.

– 3rd Yato: with several Fw-56, KB-3, KB-4 and He.72.

1st Training Orlyak (based in Kazanluk):

– 1st Yato: with DAR-9.

– 2nd Yato:?

– 3rd Yato:?

2nd Training Orlyak (based in Telish):

School of "Blind" Flight (instrumental): with Ju.52 and Fw.58.

3rd Training Orlyak (based in Stara Zagora):

1st Yato of Army: with ?.

2nd Attack Yato: with PZL.43.

3rd Fighter Yato: with ?

Technical School of NCOs (based in Kazanluk).

It also aimed to consolidate the Karlovo aerodrome as a reference center for aircraft maintenance and repair, and by mid-1941 the Lovech Technical Center (where the National Aircraft Factory or DSF, responsible for the DAR aircraft will be located).

On June 26, 443 Yato deployed its 9 S-328s to the Kavala airfield to provide air support to the "Aegean detachment" recently created by Bulgaria to control the Aegean coastal region within its national borders. Aerial reconnaissance was carried out from Thessaloniki (Solum) to Alexandroupolis (Dedeagach), but also served to allow air connections with the German neighbours, to map Bulgarian Thrace, support the ground forces, etc.

In July 1941 a new contract was signed with the Germans for the acquisition of nine second-hand but upgraded Bf.109E3 (with E4 cockpit like the ones already owned by the BAF, so its official name would be Bf.109E3a). This aircraft shipment arrived by train from Germany to Karlovo on August 23, and was immediately transferred for assembly. The name given to these aircraft in the BAF was "Strela" (arrow). After this acquisition, the number of Bf.109E would amount to 19 items, an insufficient number to provide a good air defense in Bulgarian skies.

As Nedialkov and Neulen refer, only a couple of months later there is another restructuring in the BAFs motivated by the creation of its most powerful fighter unit, the so-called Galata Orlyak (officially created in October 1941), whose core will continue to be the E models of the Bf.109 now reassigned to other aerodromes from where they will cover Black Sea coastal region the among other tasks (although supported by six of the omnipresent B.534) but with special attention to the cities of Burgas and Varna.

One special feature of the "Galata" was its swift availability to take action if they were required to do so, each Yato keeping several aircraft ready for combat from dawn until dusk. The inability for night flight, will shortly after be revealed as a handicap of the Bulgarian air defense system.

From their coastal location they would have occasion to make contact with the enemy on several occasions. In one of them, a Soviet PBY Catalina seaplane was intercepted by two Bf.109, although for technical reasons, the Bf.109 could not fire to shoot it down, so the Soviet plane escaped without any damage.

The BAR structure in October will be as it follows (according Mr. Nedialkov, Aeroflight.co.uk and Mr. Neulen sources):

Headquarters of VV based in Sofia.

Units deployed on the front line:

– Galata Fighter Orlyak (with its HQ at the Chayka seaplane base):

1st Fighter Yato: with 5 Bf.109E4. Based in Balchic.

2nd Fighter Yato: with 5 Bf.109E4. Based in Sarafovo.

3rd Fighter Yato: with 6 B.534. Based in Novogradec.

– Mixed Yato:

1st Krilo (formerly belonging to the 2nd Army Polk): with 5 S-328 based Balchik.

2nd Krilo (formerly belonging to the 3rd Army Polk): with 4 S-328 based on Sarafovo.

1st Army Polk:

– 1st Reconnaissance Yato: with 12 S-328. Based in Karlovo.

– 2nd Reconnaissance Yato: with 12 S-328. Based in Karlovo.

– 113th Army Yato: with ?. Based in Skopje.

– 1 Fighter Orlyak (composed by three Yatos). Based in Karlovo:

1st Fighter Yato: with 11 B.534.

2nd Fighter Yato: with 11 B.534.

3rd Fighter Yato: with 12 B.534.

– Seaplane Yato?

2nd Army:

– 1st Reconnaissance Yato: with 12 S-328.

– 2nd Reconnaissance Yato: with 12 S-328.

– 1st Army Yato: with 12 PZL.43.

– 1st Fighter Yato: with 15 B.534.

3rd Army:

– 1st Reconnaissance Yato: with 12 S-328. Based in Yambol.

– 2nd Reconnaissance Yato: with 12 S-328. Based in Yambol.

– 333rd Army Yato: with 6 S-328. Based in Sarafovo.

– 1st Fighter Yato: with 12 B.534. Possibly based in Okop.

4th Army Polk:

– 1st Reconnaissance Yato: with 12 S-328.

– 2nd Reconnaissance Yato: with 12 S-328.

– 443rd Army Yato: with 9 S-328. Based in Kavala.

– 1st Fighter Yato: with 15 B.534.

5th Bomber Polk:

– 1st Bomber Orlyak:

Yato?: with 9 Do.17. Based in Kavala.

Yato?: with Do.17Kb1 and Do.17M. Based in Plovdiv.

– 2nd Bomber Orlyak:

Yato?: with 12 B-71. Based in Plovdiv.

Yato?: with 6 B-71. Based in Kavala.

545th Training Yato: with 12 MB-200. Based in Plovdiv.

6th Fighter Polk (based on Karlovo):

– 1st Fighter Orlyak:

1st Yato: with 10 Bf.109E4. Based in Asen.

2nd Yato: with 11 PZL.24B. Based in Asen.

– 2nd Fighter Orlyak:

3rd Yato: with 12 B.534. Based in Dabene.

4th Yato: with 12 B.534. Based in Dabene.

Transport Yato.

Liaison Yato (Yato Kurierskiego).

Training Units:

Officer Training Orlyak, based on Vrazhdebna and composed of:

– 1st Yato: with 20 Fw-44.

– 2nd Yato: with 20 Fw-44.

– 3rd Yato: with several Fw-56, KB-3, KB-4 and He.72.

1st Training Orlyak (based in Kazanluk):

– 1st Yato: with DAR-9.

– 2nd Yato:?

– 3rd Yato:?

2nd Training Orlyak (based in Telish):

School of "Blind" Flight (Instrumental) : with Ju.52 and Fw.58.

3rd Training Orlyak (based in Stara Zagora):

1st Army Yato: with ¿?.

2nd Attack Yato: with PZL.43.

3rd Fighter Yato: with ?

Technical School of NCOs (based in Kazanluk).

As we have seen, the changes are not substantial compared to the previous re-structuring of the BAF, but they are of great importance. As a final consideration, the most important unit was the Air Eskadra that was composed of the 2nd, 5th and 6th Polk.

The situation of relative tranquility in the waters of the Aegean (also controlled by Italians and Germans), allowed that by November, of the bombing units deployed in the aerodrome of Kavala some of them could be dispensed with. So from November 1only 5 Do.17M remained there, returning the rest to the aerodrome in Plovdiv. On the contrary, the Black Sea became more difficult to control day by day, since although the German ground troops were in action inside the Soviet Union, the action of the Soviet Navy every day became more visible in these waters. For this purpose, the units deployed to control these waters were reinforced by the deployment in Safarovo (from Yambol) of 6 S-328 of the 333th Yato belonging to the 3rd Army Polk.

1942

A very important fact was the German invasion of the USSR in 1941, in which Bulgaria refused to participate. Germany had to accept it, but since then, all supplies of aircraft from the Reich would be severely diminished and slowed down, with only four aircraft delivered from JANUARY to September 1942. National aircraft production would play a more prominent role, but the production focused on no longer first-class fighters, which led BAF became obsolete at the most critical moment of the war, as the Americans begin to appear in the Bulgarian skies.

At the beginning of 1942 the war situation in the European theatre was in a fairly stable situation in the Balkan region, only clouded occasionally by the overflights of some British and American reconnaissance aircraft. Bulgaria asked Germany to obtain some night fighters to defend themselves from them, but because of the Reich's policy towards Bulgaria after the Russian affair, that request was completely ignored. But those reconnaissance flights were no more than the tip of the iceberg of what was to come, from June 1942 the USAF bombers based in North Africa would begin to carry out raids mainly destined to end the oil production at the refineries in the Romanian city of Ploiesti (the first took place on the 12th of that month). Ploiesti was where a great amount of the oil that the Reich demanded for its warlike activity was supplied. Of the ways to reach Ploiesti, each bomber used Bulgarian airspace like a "highway", which from the beginning began to receive part of the total tonnage of bombs they carried (as happened in the towns of Skopie, Gorna Oriahovica, Ruse and Pernik).

A number of night flights were also carried out by the Allies in the region of Macedonia mainly (although generally on the Balkans) carrying out "special operations". Faced with this nocturnal aerial activity, the BAF was completely tied hand and foot because of its inability to fly at night. Although night fighters were requested from the Reich, as we know, the answer was invariably negative.

The problem posed by these Allied bombing missions in the Balkans lay in how ill-equipped the Bulgarian aviation was to deal with the hordes of bombers accompanied by their escort fighters. This fact did not go unnoticed to the Germans, who noted that Bulgarian skies were poorly defended against the transit of hundreds of bombers; really it was a back door into Southern Europe that they had to close. The obsolete aircraft of Polish or Czech origin and even those of German origin that the Bulgarians owned, could do little in the face of this powerful enemy.

The dangerous situation in which the country's capital and other strategic points of the country were located, determined a new deployment of the fighter forces, which were as it follows:

A Fighter Orlyak was repositioned from Karlovo to Sofia. Yato 622 with 7 B.534 passed to Vrazhdebna Airport on 22 June; and Yato 612 with another seven B.534 passed to Bozhuriste. There would be available on alert during daylight hours to the different units, which will always have at least four aircraft ready to take off in no more than 5 minutes, as well as another four in 15 minutes. And even though the whole city was covered, it was the west and southwest of the city that were most heavily guarded by air patrols.

Finally, during this year, came the nationalization of the Kaproni-Bulgarski (its full name was Samoletna Fabrika Kaproni Bulgarski or SFKB), with the consequent change of denomination; now being called DSF Kasanlak. So, it was a branch of the Darzhavna Samoletna Fabrika or DSF (State Aircraft Factory) whose main plant, as we remember, was in Lovech. To maintain the functionality of the Kasanlak DSF the Italian staff who worked on it and of course the chief designers (Picini and Caligaris) stayed in their works.

The framework of the BAF remained similar to the one existing in the previous year, so we will not explain it again.

1943

Since the beginning of this year, the aviation factories of Kazanluk and Lovech, the main maintenance facility of Karlovo and Skopie, have come under the jurisdiction of the Ministry of War Supplies and Maintenance Department. It also commissioned the Kazanluk DSF industry to manufacture German licensed gliders to begin the training process for new pilots. This step taken by the Government of Bulgaria was very important, but like everything during the conflict, the decision made was too late to bring real solutions to its air force in the hard confrontations that had to suffer those years.

The air activities of the Americans in Bulgarian skies continued during this year and in addition the bombings against Bulgarian targets began (Sofia mainly), and the only airplane moderately suitable that Bulgaria could oppose the Americans with was the Bf.109E, that for this moment, but obsolete compared to any plane that could face. In addition, as Bulgaria had become a second category ally of the Axis (due to its limited military activity up to that time), this resulted into a persistent

The obsolete Do.11 Ds showing the BAF Coat of arms used from 1937 to 1941. It was known as "Prilep" (bat) and served from 1937 until 1940 as first line units, until being replaced by the more modern Do.17. [From Public Domain]

The He-51 fighters of German origin were soon relegated to advanced training missions. In 1936 the commercial relations between Germany and Bulgaria were increasing in the arrival of airplanes that began to become obsolete in the Reich as the He-51. [From Public Domain]

A brand new DAR-3a plane made in Bulgaria. Local planes manufacturing never could fullfill the BAF objetives in this matter. [From Public Domain]

A PZL P.24B for Bulgaria during trials at Okecie. The colors on the rudder are angled. [Kagero Archives]

The PZL P.24B after frozen snow in the wheel fairings caused the plane to flip over on landing. [Kagero Archives]

An unarmed P.24B No. 1-22 without its canopy. [Kagero Archives]

PZL P.24B's in Bulgaria without canopies or wheel fairings. [Kagero Archives]

PZL P.24B No. 2-11 with canopy and wheel fairings. [Kagero Archives]

A PZL P.24B. [Kagero Archives]

Five P.24B's with No. 4 and squadron nos. 11 and 22 at Bozhurishte. [Kagero Archives]

PZL P.24B No. 1-11 during the naming ceremony. [Kagero Archives]

Several crews pose in front of and over a PZL.43. About 50 units of this attack plane were acquired by the BAF. Actually they were the Polish made PZL.23 whose export version was called PZL.43. [Courtesy of Stephan Boshniakov]

In spite of its limitations Ar.65 represented a step forward in the formation of a modern air force in Bulgaria, although due to its obsolescense it was used as advanced trainer as soon as 1937. [Courtesy of Carmel Attard]

The obsolete MB.200 was used in Bulgaria as a trainer for bombers. In this picture we can see a French plane but similar to what the Bulgarians acquired. [From Public Domain]

A Bf.109E waits in Safarovo aerodrome before its departure towards a new mission during 1941. From this airbase, Black Sea waters were controlled by the Bulgarians against Soviet Navy. [Courtesy of Rod´s Warbird]

The unmistakably stylized silhouette of the D.520 with Bulgarian badges. It was armed with a powerful 20 mm cannon and 4 7.9 mm machine guns. [Courtesy of Rod´s Warbird]

A Bulgarian Dornier Do.17 rests next to a German Junkers Ju.52/3m on an unknown Bulgarian airfield. In spite of their importance as transport during WW2, Bulgaria only purchased about seven Ju.52/3m. [Courtesy of Rod´s Warbird]

A Yugoslavian Dornier Do.17K that a few months later will carry Bulgarian insignia.
[Courtesy of Rod´s Warbird]

One of the first air rivals of the BAF, the Yugoslavian Bf.109E. Here we can see several Bf.109E before
to deliver them to Yugoslavia. [Courtesy of ASISBIZ]

Picture of a Dornier Do.17K bomber of the Royal Yugoslavian Air Force as those who would join
the BAF in a few months. [Courtesy of Rod´s Warbird]

Crews of the Bulgarian Bomber Arm pose for a picture in front of a Do.17. When this aircraft joined the BAF, Bulgarian bombing capabilities increased significantly. There were two sources where the Bulgarian got this plane: purchasing Do.17 M from Germany and capturing Dornier Do.17K from the Royal Yugoslavian Air Force. [Courtesy of Stephan Boshniakov]

One man posing besides a Avia B-135 aircraft. Bulgaria tried to build with license 50 of this obsolete fighter under the name of DAR-11 "Lyastovitsa" (swallow), but at the end this plan was cancelled. [Courtesy of Georgi from Bibliotekata]

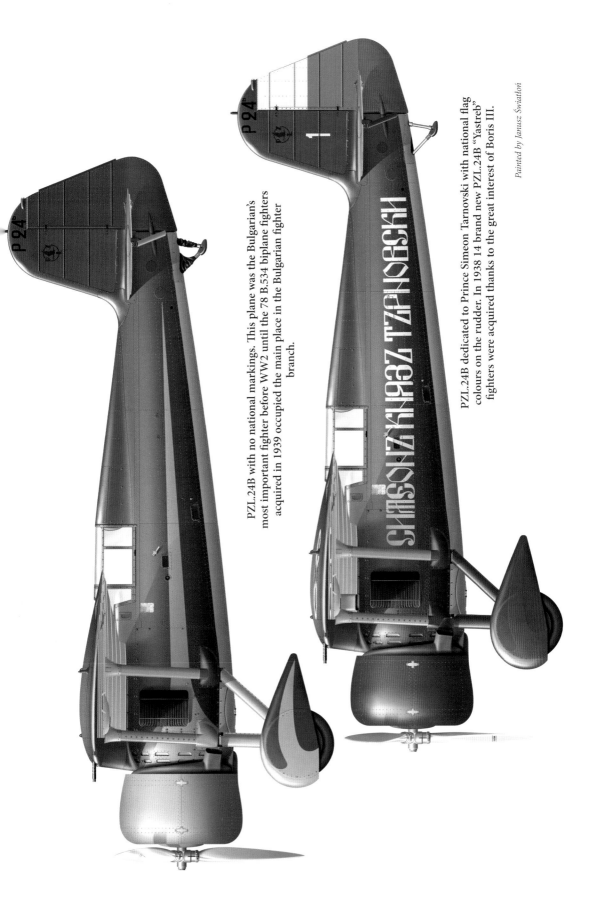

PZL.24B with no national markings. This plane was the Bulgarian's most important fighter before WW2 until the 78 B.534 biplane fighters acquired in 1939 occupied the main place in the Bulgarian fighter branch.

PZL.24B dedicated to Prince Simeon Tarnovski with national flag colours on the rudder. In 1938 14 brand new PZL.24B "Yastreb" fighters were acquired thanks to the great interest of Boris III.

Painted by Janusz Światłoń

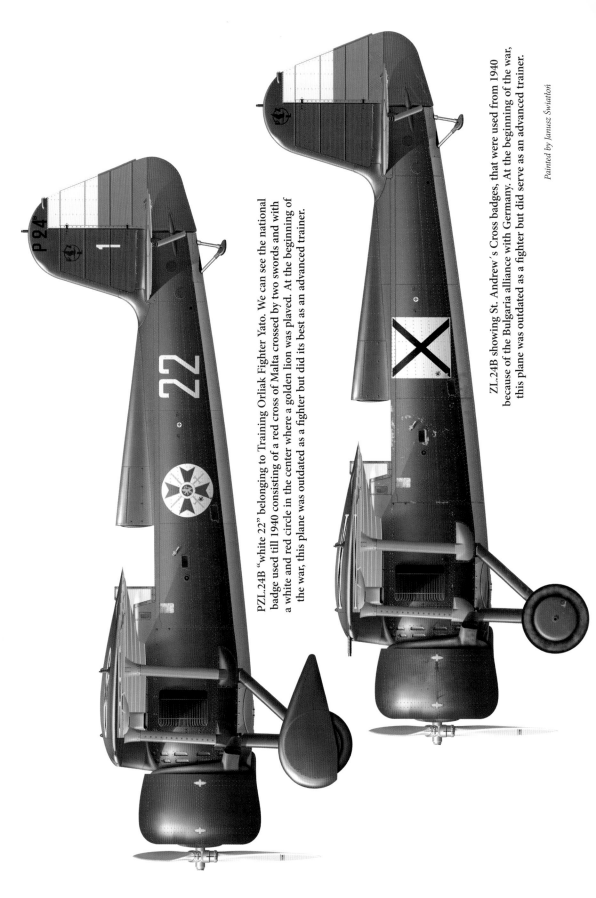

PZL.24B "white 22" belonging to Training Orliak Fighter Yato. We can see the national badge used till 1940 consisting of a red cross of Malta crossed by two swords and with a white and red circle in the center where a golden lion was plaved. At the beginning of the war, this plane was outdated as a fighter but did its best as an advanced trainer.

ZL.24B showing St. Andrew´s Cross badges, that were used from 1940 because of the Bulgaria alliance with Germany. At the beginning of the war, this plane was outdated as a fighter but did serve as an advanced trainer.

Painted by Janusz Światłoń

lack of spare parts for the aircraft, and that is the reason why many aircraft of the BAF were not in working order.

This critical situation in the Bulgarian skies came to be improved thanks to the action of Germany. The Eastern Front increasingly demanded more and more troops and more Luftwaffe aircraft that necessarily had to leave more distant areas neglected as was the case of Bulgaria. These events unfolded because the FAB's imperative need to obtain more aircraft led Bulgaria to negotiate with other countries about this matter.

According to Nedialkov and Neulen, in February 1943 talks were held with the government of the Vichy France with the aim of acquiring Bloch MB.152 fighters in exchange for Bulgarian tobacco. Negotiations were under way, but Germany refused to move forward. Understanding that it was necessary to reinforce the FAB (the spearhead of the fighters were Bf.109E and the already venerable B.534), in March Germany offered the Bulgarians the D.520 fighter, also French, which they had in abundant quantity as war booty. At first, the number of aircraft would be 120 (with spare parts included) and would reinforce the existing pact between both countries. From Sofia's Government the green light was given to the operation, although at first only 100 aircraft were ordered (of which only 96 arrived in Bulgaria). For the preparation of the Bulgarian pilots to the new French fighter, about 40 pilots were sent to Nancy (in France) where the German training unit JG 107 was based, which had the same aircraft. In Nancy the Bulgarian pilots would carry out advanced train-ing with the D.520, effectively achieving their conversion to the new fighter model. The D.520 that after the invasion of France, happened to be controlled by Germany, were systematically used in training units. Although they were not the most modern aircraft of the timt, for Bulgaria they represented a very important advance in their Fighters units; in fact it was even considered in combat by the Luftwaffe, although its sale to Bulgaria was finally accepted.

The sale of the planes was made in August of 1943, the first arriving 48 D.520 in this same month to Bulgaria handled by Bulgarian, German and French pilots; in September of that same year the French fighters will be officially received in a ceremony made at the aerodrome of Karlovo (where the fighters would have their base). The aircraft were immediately integrated into the 6th Polk under the command of Lieutenant Colonel Valkov and distributed between their 1st and 2nd Orlyak (under the command of the Captains Russew and Boschnakow respectively). Almost immediately, two Yatos with seven aircraft each deployed near the Bulgarian capital: 612th in Vrazdebna and 622th in Bozhuriste. They began operating during November, when the D.520 were fully integrated into the defensive system of Sofia, since the mission entrusted to them would be to defend the capital from Allied bombing. However many of them were shot down mainly by the P-38 Lightning belonging to the 9th American Air Force, without being able to shot down the al-lied bombers beforehand.

Thanks to Bulgarian diplomatic "movements" and, of course, German interests, the latter would also supply Bf.109G batches (really modern models comparable to those used at the time by the Germans); 29 Model G2 of the German aircraft were the first to arrive at the Balkan country to replace the French fighters in the 2nd Orlyak. These aircraft since their arrival at 3/6 and joined the consequent conversion course of the pilots (assisted by German personnel), allowed quickly putting the G2 into active use. Their initial missions consisted of air patrols of south and south-west areas of Sofia, from their Bozhurishte and Vrazhdebna bases.

In addition to the much needed fighters, 6 Do.17M bombers, 18 modern Fw.189 reconnaissance aircraft and 12 Ar.196 seaplanes were also acquired (the latter were being negotiated since 1942).

As we mentioned before, and according to Nedialkov and Bily, in March, the facilities of DAR in Lovech received 12 B-135 fighters from the Avia factory in several containers. These aircrafts had been completed on October 6 1942, then flight tested over Czech territory, dismantled and sent to Bulgaria. Assembly, maintenance and operation instructions as well as several spare parts arrived too. Despite their arrival, these aircraft would not be operational until the following month of August, when they would begin their flight tests in Bulgaria. It would be August 28th after several tests when these aircraft were incorporated into the structure of the BAF. An important detail in these aircraft assembled in Bulgaria is that they lacked the 20 mm gun that theoretically the should have carried (being armed only with two 7.92 mm machine guns); which drastically weakened their firepower. This reason together with its low performance, the low power of the engine and the German refusal to allow Avia to produce motors or any other element that was not destined to Germany; determined on the one hand that despite having the license to produce 50 units in Bulgaria it was decided not to do so, and on the other hand that despite being completely new, the B-135 immediately became integrated in the Fighter School in Dolna Mitropoliya. The facilities provided by Germany to supply the D.520 to Bulgaria are closely related to the refusal to allow the delivery of engines for Bulgarian-made B-135s and consequently with the completion of the history of the still-born DAR- 11 (the B-135 built in Bulgaria). More D.520 would continue to be received until the beginning of the following year, so that a good number of these aircraft could always be kept operational.

As a curiosity, these B-135 aircraft were not allowed to be flown by the students in the Fighter School, being used only occasionally by the instructors. The cause was the difficulty of flying the plane to pilots without enough flying experience.

Another important step, in addition to the arrival of the Bf.109G and the D.520, was the location of the first radar units for the Early Warning Service in Bulgaria. In this way, Bulgarian aviation, although obviously subordinated to German guidelines, began to act with a slight independence, being able to assume a leading role in the air defense of its own skies. According to Mr. Neldiakov sources, Freya LS and F fixed radars were located in Chivaovci (near Sofia), Debetaky (near Lovech), Kichevo (near Varna), Kableshkovo (near Panagurishte), Sliven, Hysaria and Rasgrad. In addition, some mobile radars were also used in different locations, depending on the current situation.

As we have said, Bulgaria had become yet another target for US air forces. It was in the autumn of this year that this change of attitude of the US towards Bulgaria would be clearly seen. The purpose of these attacks, which had the capital Sofia as the main objective, was to lower the morale of the population that would lead to create political instability that could end with the departure of the Axis of Bulgaria. With Bulgaria out of the war, the Germans would have to dedicate many of their troops to control the country (the same as in Italy), troops that would be withdraw from other combat fronts where they would be much needed.

These bombings directed against the Bulgarian capital in a systematic way, consisted of ten missions carried out between November 14 1943 and APRIL 17 1944 by the US 15th Air Force based in Italy.

The arrival of the new models of Ju.87D, allowed to dedicate (at least partially) the fleet of Ju.87R towards missions of ground training for new pilots. Thus in September, 12 Ju.87R were sent to Plovdiv for this mission.

In summary, at the end of 1943, the structure of the BAF had not undergone many major modifications with respect to the previous two years (except for the disappearance of the Fighter Orlyak in Galata or Galata Fighter Orlyak), although there are variations in the material operated by the BAF, much improved especially where fighters are concerned since they joined the combat units; although it would be in 1944 when they managed to be 100% operational (according to Mr. Nedialkov, Aeroflight.co.uk and Mr. Neulen):

Training Polk, consisting of:

– 3rd Training Yato.

– Technical School of NCOs and Officers.

Transport YatoAirborne Yato: Composed by Ju.523m.

Liaison Yato: With various aircraft such as the Bf.108B1.

1st Reconnaissance Army Polk, composed by:

– 3rd Army Reconnaissance Orlyak. It had S.328, Fw.189 and CB 11.

– 73rd Long Range reconnaissance Yato with Do.17.

– Seaplanes Orlyak. Constituted mainly by He.60 and Ar.196 (these will be integrated in the 161th Coastal Surveillance Yato).

2nd Attack Polk (renamed from Army Polk to Attack Polk), composed by:

– 2nd Orlyak. Equipped with Ju.87 DR and ex-fighters B.534.

5th Bomber Polk, composed by:

– 2nd Orlyak. Equipped with Do.17 and B-71.

6th Fighter Polk, composed by:

– 3rd Orlyak. Equipped with Bf.109EG and D.520.

The 2nd, 5th and 6th Polk as we will recall, constituted the most powerful level of aerial capability in the BAF, that was the Air Eskadra.

To conclude this year, another fact related to the BAF is the creation of the first Airborne Assault Unit called "Drujina", which was created from parachute units in July 1943. The aircraft used in their operations and trainings were the omnipresent Ju.52/3m, who in addition to their role of transport, also played this role.

1944

The air battles over Bulgaria from the previous year greatly increased by the intense American military activity and several American aircraft were shot down by Bulgarians. In spite of this, the first months of the year began with the bombers making night raids that could not be answered by a day-fighter fleet such as the Bulgarian, although anti-aircraft artillery did its duty. According to Nedialkov and Neulen, after APRIL 1944, coinciding with the last massive bombing on Sofia, the Allies appeared to have a change of priorities in its activities of bombing. Now Bulgaria ceases to be of interest, with Ploiesti's oil fields once again being the prime targets of US air forces, at least until mid-August of the same year, as the Soviets were inexorably advancing on Romanian territory. Although this did not prevent some more bombing of Bulgaria, like the two that suffered the Karlovo aerodrome in June, which involved the destruction of about 80 aircraft of all types.

The period of US attacks on Bulgaria was devastating for the country. Despite the increasingly organized defense against US aircraft by both aircraft and antiaircraft artillery (which took a toll on the Americans), between APRIL 1941 and September 1944, more than 500,000 kilograms of bombs that devastated everywhere they flew over, causing the deaths of at least 1,828 people and about 2,372 injured.

The actions of the BAF were carried mainly by the Bf.109G (whose number of aircraft acquired from Germany between those of the G2 model and those of the G6 were of 145) and between August of 1943 until the coup d'etat in September 1944 the D.520 shot down 53 planes (37 heavy bombers and 16 fighters). The other strong point was the antiaircraft artillery that shot down at least 4 more bombers. In addition to the casualties in the American ranks, many other aircraft were damaged and in many cases were unable to complete their mission or return to their base unharmed. Against this, their own losses amounted to 27 fighters shot down losing 23 pilots, as well as 30 more aircraft that were damaged in combat as much as by accidents of several kinds.

Until 1944, the training of Bulgarian pilots was maintained in German Flight Schools, both in Germany (Werneuchen) and in France (Nancy, headquarters of the instructional units equipped with D.520).

A little more time had to wait so that in the proximity of the Russian "steamroller" and the great debacle that German troops were suffering every day, discontent spread like gunpowder in Bulgaria. And the result of this discontent, together with the formation of anti-German partisan groups, led to a veritable coup d'etat that took place on September 9, establishing a pro-Soviet government in Bulgaria.

The arrangement of the BAF on September 28, 1944, evidently based on what had existed until now but now commanded by the polkovnik Drenikov, is again changed as follows (the number of aircraft corresponds to those that were operational) (based on Mr. Neulen work):

Unit	Yatos	Model	Number
VV Headquarter (Sofía).	Staff Squadron	Fi.156	2
2º Attack Polk (under the command of Captain Kraivanov)			
1/2 Orlyak (Bozhuriste)	3	Ju.87D	38
2/2 Orlyak (Vrazhdebna)	1	B.534	6
5º Bomber Polk (under the command of Captain Batanov)			
1/5 Orlyak (Vrazhdebna)	2 Do.17M/P/Kb1	14	
2/5 Orlyak (Plovdiv)	2 B-71	12	
6º Fighter Polk (under the command of major Atanasov)			
1/6 Orlyak (Bozhuriste)	3	D.520	16
– 672nd Yato			
– 682nd Yato			
– 692nd Yato			
2/6 Orlyak (Vrazhdebna)	3	Bf.109G6	16
– 642nd Yato			
– 652nd Yato			
– 662nd Yato			
3/6 Orlyak (Bozhuriste)	3	Bf.109G6	19
– 612nd Yato			
– 622nd Yato			
– 632nd Yato			
1º Reconnaissance Polk (under the command of Polkovnik Sapunov)			
Command	–	Fi.156 D1	1
3/1 Orlyak (Varba)	2	Fw.189 A	14
– 333rd Yato			
– 334th Yato			
4/1 Orlyak (Bozhuriste)	2	S-328	9
–	–	KB-11	13
– 353rd Yato			
– 453rd Yato			
73rd Long Range Yato (Vrazhdebna)	–	Do.17	4
Seaplane Yato (Varna)	–	Ar.196A3	7
Transport and airborne Squadron	1	Ju.52/3m	4

The situation of the BAF that would now clash against its former German allies relied on a reduced fleet of no more than 146 (167 according to other sources) aircraft. These were divided into 53 fighters, 32 bombers, 33 light-attack/bombing aircraft and 28 reconnaissance aircraft; most of which were, at the time of the conflict, either of German manufacture or provided by them. To increase the number of aircraft available, domestic production was increased, so that about 50 KB-11 were incorporated in a short time. Their operational zone included the areas of Thrace, Macedonia and Serbia, where some fighter and aerial superiority missions would take place, although due to the Luftwaffe almost disappearing from those skies, mainly the BAF was destined to tasks of ground attack (troops and enemy communications), support for Bulgarian troops, in addition to liaison, reconnaissance or transport. During this period some B.534 had the opportunity to make nocturnal attacks against retreating Germans.

The units involved in the anti-German war activity were the components of the Air Eskadra (the Fighter Polk, Bomber and Ground Attack) along with the Reconnaissance Polk. This combative period began with the support of the BAF to the 1st and 4th Armies, and came to an end after crossing the borders of Yugoslavia, because the airbases of the BAF were very far from the front (the lack of appropriate infrastructures in the airports of Western Bulgaria contributed to not allowing appropriate Bulgarian actions against the German troops), finishing the so-called "Patriotic War" that developed the Bulgarians from the 9 of September to the 2 of December.

The BAF or VV after the coup d'etat, will be designated as VNVV and its impact in the global count of the war is 25 German destroyed aircraft and numerous ground targets destroyed or damaged. Specifically and according to Nedialkov sources, in 3,744 missions carried out, 694 armored vehicles (German motorized columns), 85 pieces of artillery, several trains (23 locomotives and 496 wagons), 16 bridges and 11 railway stations were destroyed. As can be seen, most of the missions were ground attack, making reconnaissance missions less important. On the Bulgarian side, 32 aircraft were shot down with the loss of 18 pilots and crew. Actually, this great effort sustained by the BAF took place between 9 September and 7 October. According to Nedialkov, after the Armistice signed with the Soviet Union on October 28, the actions of the BAF will decrease significantly (680 combat missions until the end of the war), due to the small number of aircraft ready to fly (about 77) and the lack of spare parts quickly reduced this number. From this moment on, the main missions would be support-reconnaissance and would be carried out by two Liaison Yato, the 73th Reconnaissance Yato and a Transport Yato.

The structure of the BAF in October 1944, already in full support of Bulgarian ground troops against the former German ally, is changed again. The changes are marked by two very significant facts; on one hand the severe wear and tear suffered by Bulgarian aircraft in fighting retreating Germans and on the other hand the

Soviet need for a Bulgarian ground force. For this latter reason, the fighter force is practically unused and replaced by the Soviets in the task of dominating the Yugoslav skies, respecting in addition to the attack aircraft, the Bulgarian transport, reconnaissance and liaison. So that in October 1944, the FABs would be presented as follows (according Mr. Nedialkov, Aeroflight.co.uk and Mr. Neulen sources):

Headquarters of VV based in Sofia.

Mixed units:

– 73th Long Range Reconnaissance Yato (Vrazhdebna) with 4 Do.17P.

– Seaplane Yato (Varna) with 7 Ar.196A3.

– Courier Yato with 3 Fi.156.

– Liaison Yato with 1 Bf.108.

– Transport Yato with 2 JU.52.

Training Units:

Orlyak Officers Training, based in Vrazhdebna and composed by:

– 1st Yato with?

– 2nd Yato with?.

– 3rd Yato with ¿?.

Air Training Polk

– **1st Training Orlyak** (based in Kazanluk):

1st Yato with DAR-9

2nd Yato with?

3rd Yato with?

– **2nd Training Orlyak** (based in Telish):

School of Flight Instrumental or "blind."

– **3rd Training Orlyak** (based in Stara Zagora):

1st Army Yato: ?.

2nd Attack Yato: with PZL.43.

3rd Fighter Yato: ?

Technical School of NCOs (based in Kazanluk).

1945

After the so-called "Patriotic War", the BAF was completely exhausted. They had stopped receiving new aircraft a long time before, but the continued use of them and the absence of spare materials led to a very limited number of aircraft still in operational conditions by the beginning of 1945. Since then, and with the restructuring of the BAF that would take place along Soviet lines, they will try to drop all German planes and replace them by Soviet-made designs like Yak-9M, Il-23M and Pe-2. Bulgaria moved from the German sphere to Soviet the sphere, and BAF was a good example.

Any other air support activity for Bulgarian infantry and armoured troops in the front would be carried out by the 17th Soviet Air Force, limiting Bulgarian aircraft to their 1st Army with two Fi.156 and a Bf.108 based in Zemun.

CHAPTER III

Fighter Units

If there is a branch within the BAF that has taken only fame for the Bulgarian aviation in the Second World conflict, it is the fighter branch. This is not strange, since the limited action of Bulgarian troops beyond their borders and their refusal to intervene on the Eastern front, reduced the activity of the whole BAF. But the fighter branch had its days of glory motivated by the Allied change of strategy for the Balkans. Since the day that the town of Ploiesti (in Romania) was chosen as the destination for thousands of tons of Allied bombs, Bulgaria became the route that, first from North Africa and later from Italian bases, would be used by the USAF and RAF. In the fact of these hordes of hundreds of bombers and fighters, only the fighter units could oppose, so they had to update material and be ready to face that difficult challenge.

Although there were a lot of clashes between defenders and attackers in Bulgarian skies, we report below the main actions of the Bulgarian fighters throughout the conflict, both with and against the Axis; there were many more small clashes against enemy planes that people interested in the matter can read in the superb works of Mr. Neldiakov, but in order to make the reading easier, we have omitted them. We mainly follow the works of Mr. Nedialkov, Mr. Neulen, Mr. Boshniakov, Mr. Mandjukov , Mr. Safarík and Mr. Muchovsky in order to plot a timeline of events, although works from other authors have been used too; trying to show the most accurate figures despite the disparity (on occasion) of these data in the different sources.

Summer 1939

During the summer of 1939 the Bulgarian Air Force continued its process of enhancing its air power. As far as fighter units were concerned, let us remember that B.534 biplanes were acquired. Despite being outdated at the time, they represented progress in terms of what existed in the Bulgarian aircraft fleet. These arrived packed by rail to Karlovo, from where they were integrated into the 2nd Orlyak Istrebitelen (2nd Fighter Regiment). The aircraft were deployed at the Karlovo and Vrazhdebna airfields, where they remained until the attack on Yugoslavia (and the subsequent response by these), forcing a redeployment of several air units. So after the Serbian attack on Kjustendil, west of Sofia, the 2nd Orlyak Istrebitelen was sent and assigned to the aerodrome of Bozhuriste.

Spring 1941

With the deployment of some air units in Bulgarian territory due to the invasion of Yugoslavia and Greece by the Axis, there was a new redeployment, in this case motivated by the occupation of part of Yugoslavia and Greece by Bulgarian forces. It was necessary to "take possession" of these territories demonstrating who the new owners were, while optimizing the air forces for the whole of the new national territory. In spite of this, the main air bases where the majority of Bulgarian units were deployed remained the ones located inside the Bulgarian borders prior to the annexation of the new territories.

Another highlight of the tranquility of the Bulgarian fighter forces during this period was the transfer of some fighters to the Chaika channel air base near Varna, where 10 Bf.109E4 (from 682 and 692 Yatos) and 6 B.534 were deployed, under the codename "Galata Orlyak". These planes were based in Novogradec, Balchik and Buhovci, from where they would be responsible for the air defense of the Bulgarian shores of the Black Sea that was of vital importance because it was a very important supply route for the Axis.

1942

In spite of having an internal combat front against the partisans fundamentally in the annexed territories, as far as the fighter units the period from 1941 until the middle of 1943 would pass pleasurably without having to be involved in situations of combat. Bulgaria was far from any open front of combat and therefore the danger of being involved in it. In spite of this and as mentioned, there were various modifications in the structure of the BAF, which in the end left the ubiquitous air bases of Vrazhdebna and Bozhurishte as the main ones within the air defense of the country.

1 August 1943

This date would be a milestone for the Bulgarian pilots, as Operation "Tidal Wave" began, which consisted of massive air strikes by US four-engined bombers at the Ploiesti oil installations in Romania (comprising nine refineries, oil, diesel, gasoline and derivative storage) arranged in an area that covered 50 square kilometers. In this operation, Bulgaria acted merely as a route for the bombers. These aircraft belonged to the US 9th Air Force and they were under the command of Major General Louis Brerkton. The planes had departed from Africa, specifically from Benghazi (on the present Libyan coast) and following a northern course they reached the border area between Greece and Albania, crossing Bulgarian Macedonia and north-west Bulgaria then toward Ploiesti (in southern Romania). The crossing of Bulgarian airspace occurred between 12:30 and 13:15 hours through the "corridor" west of the Slivnica-Archar line, according to Nedialdov.

But this large-scale incursion consisting of at least some 166 B-24s (some sources raise this to 177 or 178), which departed at 8:00 am on Sunday, August 1, from Benghazi, did not go unnoticed by the German surveillance centers that were located with the radar in Greece while still flying over the Mediterranean. The radar on Mount Vitosha detected the more than 160 bombers entering Bulgarian territory on their route to the northeast. At that time the basis of Bulgarian air defense relied mainly on the old B.534 (lacking radio equipment and oxygen) and some Bf.109.

Upon receiving the alarm signal at 12:15 a.m., the two main fighter bases intended for such a mission were set in motion. About 12:25–12:30 six B.534 fighters from the 612th Yato based in Vrazhdebna took off, under Lieutenant Martin Petrov's command; while another four B.534 belonging to the 622th Yato, under the command of Lieutenant Rusi Rusev, did the same from the aerodrome of Bozhurishte. In the same moment but from the aerodrome of Karlovo, another ten fighters also took off to face the adversary; they were Bf.109G-2 from the 6th Orlyak (specifically from 3/6). The Messerschmitt fighters took off in three small formations, the first consisting of three aircraft under Lieutenant Grigorov command, the second of three planes under Lieutenant Kondakov command departed five minutes later and finally four aircraft under Lieutenant Stoyanov command.

Both formations of B.534 met in the air over the city of Berkouista, to the north of Sofia. Together they tried to approach the last wave of American bombers which were hurrying towards Romania. Of all the planes that took off in search of the Americans, only one of them (a B.534) could make visual contact with the enemy over the Danube River. The situation was evident, the B-24s were flying quite high compared to the height of the B.534 fighters (this height allowed American bomber formations to fly over the Bulgarian mountain regions) and the limited power of the B .534 prevented any attempt to search and reach for the swift bombers. Because of this situation and the impossibility of reaching them, the possibility that they use the same route on their return trip from the Romanian oil fields was suggested, so that following the orders of their flight leaders they flew quickly to their aerodromes for refueling. And once again the aircraft, on the return trip of the B-24, would wait for them to the right height trying to put this situation in their favor. Although not all Bulgarian planes returned to their starting bases, for example Stoyanov, who landed in Vrazhdebna.

After the bombing of Ploiesti and some other nearby areas, about 15.00 the bombers set course back over Bulgaria. Now there were four B.534 that took off from Bozhurishte, seven did the same from Vrazhdebna and four Bf.109 led by the future ace porutzyk Stoyan Stoyanov took off from Vrazhdebna.

According to the Bulgarian planning, B.534 biplanes which had a very slow climb speed (the first major problem for Czechoslovakian fighters), would have eliminated that problem by waiting for the B-24 on their return flight, at its highest altitude. According to Nedialkov and Neulen, finally they spotted the Americans between the towns of Vratza and Ferdinand, where the first fighting took place at a height of about 3,000 meters. Seven B.534 intercepted 18 B-24 and fired their weapons but without results. At this moment, the second major problem of Avia biplanes, their speed, came to light. This was only slightly higher than that of the bombers, so the opportunities to get into firing position should be made the most of, since once that moment passed, the next could only be achieved after a long period of time. But they succeeded, and the B.534 formation again managed to position itself for a new attack; this happened in the area of Kjustenil, after about 150 km of pursuit to get back to shooting. The brave Bulgarian pilots launched themselves against the well-defended formation of B-24. Bombers without escort fighters could be a bit easier target if they had encountered faster fighters, but against which this kind of Bulgarian planes, would be a very hard bone to gnaw. And here is the third big problem of the B.534, since in attacking the B-24, the machine guns they had were too small a caliber to really cause devastating effects on those big monsters. So the damage inflicted on the Americans was completely surmountable by them, who, in exchange, returned the welcome they received with an intense machine gun fire response that damaged several fighters that had to make forced landings.

The bombers that managed to reach Ploiesti, evidently were not the same ones that returned, since the mentioned 166 were subjected to a fierce defensive fire by the German anti-aircraft guns, in addition to the action of the Luftwaffe and the Romanian aviation (that had been directed towards the Allied formation through the Balkan air control center). All this situation meant that the return of the bombers was not just as methodically organized as was the outward flight, since these were dispersed in wide sectors within its flight route, that passed through the skies of western Bulgaria. So at 3:00 p.m., the bombers began to return, with damage of varying extent in many of them and with scarce fuel for the return in all the B-24 bombers.

At that moment there were already at about 6,500 feet high two formations of B.534 (one with four aircraft from Bozhuriste and the other with seven coming from Vrazhdebna), that after failing in their attempt to hunt them in their route towards

Ploiesti, now tried to close as far as possible the route of flight of the bombers in the direction of neighboring Yugoslavia, waiting for them in the area of Ossogovaska Planina. Again the biplanes were matched with several Bf.109. In particular the four fighters under Lieutenant Stoyan Stoyanov's command (the four planes took off from Vrazhdebna at 15:10 in two pairs: the first commanded by Stoyanov with Bonev as wingman, and the second commanded by Krastev and Bochev as wingman). The first couple would head north, where they contacted 16 B-24s over Ferdinand (now called Montana) and the Bulgarian pilots attacked. The second pair also found their enemies (specifically 4 B-24) over the town of Varshec, where they engaged them. Also the Bulgarian anti-aircraft defense could participate as much as possible in the attack against the B-24, shooting down three of them during the return flight of the Americans.

Despite the initial advantage of the Bulgarian aircraft over the Americans, this was relative since the low speed and the limited range of action of the biplanes, compared with B-24 would only allow them to make one attack or with good luck strafing them twice. Fortunately for the Bulgarians, the Bf.109 were able to act against the Americans in the direction of the Yugoslav border, even flying over Macedonian territory.

The B.534 already waiting at height began to locate diverse groups of bombers trying to join in "ad hoc" formations coming from the north. The area where the biplanes met the Americans was located between the cities of Vratza and Ferdinand, the engagements occurring at about 3,000 meters height. The B.534 from Vrazhdebna took advantage of their better height, they flew against the enemy formations making use of all its armament (too light for bombers as strongly protected as the B-24), to finally arrive at very low height after taking control again of their planes. They immediately tried to get back into firing position despite the very modest speed of the fighters with respect to the bombers. In spite of this, after a long time they were able to make another attack (approximately over the town of Kjustenil), with a similar result, since they achieved many impacts on the bombers but with little general damage on them.

The return to their aerodromes was not so triumphant since some of the B.534 were definitely damaged during landing.

As a result of all the air combat that day in Bulgarian skies, five bombers (four according to Neldiakov) were shot down by the Messerschmitt fighters and none by the B.534. Two of them were shot down by the future Bulgarian ace, Lieutenant Stoyan Stoyanov (leader of the formation of Bf.109) and one each by the following pilots: Bochev, Bonev and Krastev. This action was worth to Stoyanov to receive the Cross for Bravery by king Boris III, as also happened with Bochev. Even a pair of B.534 pilots who, although they did not shoot down any planes, were decorated for their brave harassment of the enemy. Also the following month in the German embassy the new heroes received the German Iron Cross in the embassy of this country in Sofia.

On the other hand, the action against the bombers had left another lesson for the BAF: there was not adequate preparation by the air defense units against situations of this kind, which would also be repeated later (as in fact happened). For this reason the training of the pilots was increased for the coming actions with conversion courses for the same.

It is also necessary to note that several bombers returned to their Mediterranean bases quite damaged by the fire received in both the Romanian and Bulgarian skies, but in spite of this they managed to make it safe and sound.

12 August 1943

The serious situation of helplessness of the Bulgarian air force after the incidents of 1 August of 1943, determined that 3/6 (composed at that time of 16 Bf.109G2) was deployed at the aerodrome of Bozhurishte with the purpose of protecting the city of Sofia against any attack by the Allies (as its main mission). But not only the best Bulgarian fighters would receive this mission, since the anti-aircraft artillery that defended the capital, received (from the summer until the end of 1943) up to 56 8.8 cm guns of German origin.

21 October 1943

A couple of leading fighters deployed in Skopje during a patrol were confronted with a formation of 20 P-38s that were attacking the Skopje train station. Evidently, the possibilities of the two Bf.109E7 of bringing down all American fighters would not happen. But at least, they tried to disperse the enemy formation with their brave attack. The result was a P-38 damaged by the leader of the pair, podporuchik Grigorov; not realizing that this P-38 finally fell to earth. His wingman, Kamenov kept exchange of shots but without obvious any result.

Systemic bombing of Sofia

From JANUARY 1943 the Allies had in mind to put pressure on Bulgaria by systematic bombing to force them to leave the Axis. The encounter that took place in the Bulgarian skies on 1 August occurred only because it was the route of the B-24 and not to seek any confrontation with Bulgarian fighters. But the implementation of this plan had to be delayed several months due to the difficulty of launching this attack from the North African air bases. It would be from November 1, 1943 when the US 15th Air Force began to operate from its Italian base at Foggia and then began the massive bombing of Bulgaria, intended mainly in the destruction of its capital. There were ten large-scale bombings of Sofia and other Bulgarian locations, carried out by the US 15th Air Force during the day and by 205 Group RAF at night, which took place from November 14, 1943 to 17 of APRIL of 1944.

But despite having a lot of problems, the Bulgarian air defense system was learning from its mistakes and despite its limitations was refined to show its worth in the following attacks. Bulgaria discovered that if the daytime air defense of the country was neglected, nightlife simply did not exist, which the British knew how to take advantage of it very well. Despite this and during the cycle of systematic bombardment of Sofia, only 2% of the enemy planes (39) were knocked down in exchange for the loss of 14 of its own aircraft. The change of Allied strategic objectives in the Balkan region, now again against Ploiesti, was what prevented the destruction from the sky of Bulgaria was absolute; although there were still some sporadic air strikes over Bulgarian soil. Let's see how those intense days of fighting took place in those five months from November 1943 to APRIL 1944.

14 November 1943

On November 14, as we said, the Allied air campaign against Bulgaria began. There were 90 B-25 medium bombers escorted by about 100 P-38 escort fighters (49 according to Neldiakov). These approached in two waves to the Bulgarian capital an approximate height of 5,000 meters. Although once again the two fighters in Skopie were the first to launch against the intruders (without being able to locate them), it was again demonstrated how ineffective the air warning system was, since when they were warned of the alert and the 3/6 aircraft from Bozhurishte were able to take off, it was only at the moment that the bombers had already released their deadly cargos over Sofia. Despite not having avoided the bombing, at least 13 Bf.109G2 managed to contact the enemy as they retreated, although with little effectiveness since only one victory in combat could be registered, a P-38 that would fall near the locality of Debar (according to Neldiakov, this victory would be achieved by a Bf.109E7 that had left next to its pair from the airport of Skopie to intercept the intruders). In exchange, a Bf.109G2 was lost with his pilot, and two more aircraft were damaged. The tactics used by the Bulgarian pilots to attack alone or in a pair allowed a better response by the allied defensive system in their formations of fighters and bombers.

From Vrazhdebna six D.520 of the 2/6 took off, although perhaps they did not manage to make contact with the enemy.

The very positive result of the bombardment with almost no effective response by the Bulgarian fighter force and antiaircraft artillery (more than 3,500 projectiles of different calibers were fired without noting any downing), encouraged even more the Allies to carry out more bombings and with even greater forces in the days to come.

24 November 1943

This day a formation of B-24 of the US 15th Air Force (60 according to Nedialkov) escorted by the omnipresent P-38 (at least 35), again directed their blows towards Sofia. In front of them, 13 Bf.109G2 from 3/6 took off (from Bozhurishte) and quite possibly from Vrazhdebna 24 brand new D.520, in addition to the two Bf.109E7 fighters on alert from Skopje. The French-built fighters did not make contact with the enemy, but those of German origin according to some sources, managed to shoot down two B-24 and one P-38 (or only two B-24), in exchange for a Messerschmitt shot down and three damaged (these three made emergency landings). The two B-24 shot down have to be awarded to the formation leader, Captain Toplodolski. Despite these facts, the BBC itself acknowledged the loss of ten bombers in this attack (from a total of 16 aircraft lost), so it will be very difficult to ever know what really happened that day. Although at least the pilots who make contact with the enemy were arranged in two formations so that while one was thrown against the fighters (forcing them to the southwest over the Pernik Valley), the other could deal with the bombers. This tactic allowed Bulgarian pilots to obtain promising results despite the small number of Bulgarian aircraft.

So on this day perhaps the most positive fact for the Bulgarians, was not to have shot down some enemy aircraft, but thanks to the aircraft and the antiaircraft artillery (that according to Nedialkov fired 585 projectiles, mainly of large caliber), the result was that only 17 bombers were able to drop the bombs at their targets by forcing many of them to turn around; which in the end was the main mission of the Bulgarian pilots and artillery gunners.

10 December 1943

On this day, the French-built D.520 fighter had its baptism of fire against about 60 P-38s escorting several B-24s (31 according Neulen) heading towards Sofia. Quickly 17 Bf. 109 from 3/6 took off from Bozhurishte towards them in conjunction with 6 or 8 D.520 from 2/6 from Vrazhdebna (most likely also joined to the defender's force 16 D.520 from 1/6 based on Karlovo), intercepting the Americans although losing one pilot that was shot down; Captain Lazarov (according to other sources Captain Pavlov, 652nd Yato from 2/6) who had been the one to guide the D.520's frontal attack against Americans. Aircraft of French origin suffered throughout the combat from a precarious radio communication system, which failed continuously.

On the part of the Bf.109, that were the first to contact the enemy, the pilots' functions were divided, with 672nd and 682nd Yatos attacking the bombers and the 692nd Yato attacking the fighters; this being the situation that first D.520 in arriving (belonged to the 662nd Yato) found.

The main ace in the BAF Stoyan Stoyanov, with at least 4 confirmed victories and 5 damaged aircraft. During a lot of clashes against enemy planes he demonstrated his skill in attacking them. [Courtesy of ASISBIZ]

Poor quality but very interesting image showing the ace Stoyan Stoyanov close to his Bf-109E in 1943. This was the first high-level fighter in the BAF. The arrival of the Bf.109G and the D.520 in 1943 together with the Bf-109E very much improved Bulgarian air power. [Courtesy of ASISBIZ]

A couple of BAF Bf-109E7 in formation flying over Bulgarian territory in 1941. The Orlyak Galata created in October 1941 covered the coastal region with the Black Sea among other tasks. [Courtesy of ASISBIZ]

Several Bulgarian pilots form up in front of a Bf-109G2 in 1945, already showing the change of side of Bulgaria, although we can still see the St Andrew´s Cross emblem under the wing of the plane. [Courtesy of ASISBIZ]

Close-up of a pilot close to his D.520, where we can see the air intake and the elegant lines of this fighter. Although Bulgaria requested the Reich the French fighter Bloch MB.152, they only agreed to supply the also valuable D.520. [Courtesy of Stephan Boshniakov]

Several Bf.109G wait in the aerodrome the moment to take action. At last Bulgaria had a first level fighter, but the Bulgarian skies was already dominated by USAF planes.
[Courtesy of Rod´s Warbird]

Bf.109E7 wearing the insignia used by BAF since 1941. The E model of this wonderful fighter were armed with 2 cannon 20 mm and 2 7.92 mm machine guns. [Courtesy of Rod´s Warbird]

A Bf.109E4 ready to take action at the Balchik airfield. From this airbase on the northern Bulgarian Black Sea coast they can fullfill their mission of air protection of Axis convoys on the Black Sea. [Courtesy of Rod´s Warbird]

Close-up of Bf.109G6 –white seven- belonging to 3rd Orliak of the 6th Polk. This plane was armed with 2 20 mm cannon and 2 13 mm machine guns. [Courtesy of Rod´s Warbird]

Since the arrival of the first units, the Bf.109G became the spearhead of the BAF, as it was in other Axis countries as Hungary, Romania, Finland, Italy or Germany.
[Courtesy of Rod´s Warbird]

Bf.109G squadron in training flight during the performance of a mission. Bulgarian HQ considered as a very important item a very good training of the pilots, but the War prevented fullfilling this objetive. [Courtesy of Rod´s Warbird]

The incorporation to BAF of the D.520 was an important boost to its air defense potential, although this plane was rejected by German Luftwaffe as a fighter or fighter-bomber. That was the reason why D.520s went to Bulgaria and Italy. [Courtesy of Rod´s Warbird]

A pair of Bulgarian Bf.108 flying in formation. BAF Only purchased six of this wonderful liaison-trainer plane in 1940. [Courtesy of Rod´s Warbird]

A couple of Bf.109G6 belonging to the 672nd yato flying over Mount Rila. [Courtesy of Rod´s Warbird]

A row of Bf.109E awaits its moment to take action. This plane had very good flying characteristics but in the last years of the war it was surpassed by more modern fighters. [Courtesy of Rod´s Warbird]

A Bf.109G prepares to take off from an airfield covered with snow. The bad weather conditions didn´t help either defenders or attackers. [Courtesy of Rod´s Warbird]

Several Bulgarian military inspectors pose for a photo close to a German Fi.156. This plane was later was acquired by Bulgaria, who used it for reconnaissance and liaison with great success.
[Courtesy of Georgi from Bibliotekata]

Another photo taken when the German Fi.156 "Storch" was showing its capabilities to the Bulgarian delegation. They were pleasantly surprised with the behaviour of the airplane in the air.
[Courtesy of Georgi from Bibliotekata]

Two Bf.109E belonging to "Galata" Orlyak. This unit created in October 1941 was the most powerful Bugarian fighter unit at that moment, and the E models of the Bf.109 were its main plane, being B.534 fighters used too. [Courtesy of Stephan Boshniakov]

One special feature of the Bf.109E "Galata" Orlyak was its swift availability to take action if they were required to do so, each Yato keeping several aircraft ready for combat from dawn until dusk covering the Black Sea coastal region. [Courtesy of Stephan Boshniakov]

Bf.108 "white 5" bearing the yellow quick identification markings on the cowling, underwing tips and rudder. Only a few of this superb aeroplane were acquired by Bulgaria that used them integrated in the Yuri Kurierskiego Yato (Liaison Yato).

Bf.108 bearing St. Andrew's Cross and Bulgarian colors on the rudder. Although used as a liaison plane, after the Bulgarian change of side, Bf.108 would continue in service until the end of 1944 or beginning of 1945 giving support to Bulgarian ground forces against the Germans.

Painted by Arkadiusz Wróbel

Bf.109 E4 "white 4" belonging to Galata Orlyak. The "Strela" was the first modern fighter that the BAF could acquire from Germany in 1941. The main front where this plane was used was in the Black Sea coastal region.

Bf.109 E4 "white 19" belonging to Galata Orlyak. Note the special camouflage of yellow over green. The Bf.109 model E had a powerful armament consisting of two 20 mm cannon and two 7.92 mm machine gun.

Painted by Arkadiusz Wróbel

Bf.109 G6 "white 7" from 3/6 Orlyak. This plane shows the white Theater band in the aft of the fuselage and under the wing tips while it carries the St. Andrew´s Cross. That would date the plane between September 1944 and January 1945.

Bf.109 G6 "red 6" belonging to 652nd Yato from 2/6 Orlyak based in Vrazhdebna, December 20 1943. Its pilot, Lieutenant Marinopolski shot down a B-24 on that date while defending Sofia. We can see in detail the unit emblem.

Painted by Arkadiusz Wróbel

Bf.109 E3a "white 1" Only 19 Model E planes were acquired during 1940-1941; in this profile we can see one of the survivors in 1945 bearing the new white, red and green insignia, used in six positions and on the rudder. The Bulgarian Bf.109s remained in active service until 1946.

Bf.109 G6 "white 5" This plane has the new roundel that replaced the St. Andrew´s Cross in 1945 and Bulgarian flag colors on the rudder. After the Bulgarian change of side the activities of the Bulgarian fighter branch would be paralyzed, except in specific cases of reconnaissance over enemy troops, to focus on the tasks of escort and ground attack.

Painted by Arkadiusz Wróbel

According to Nedialkov the antiaircraft artillery after firing 941 shots only managed to damage one bomber but without destroying it. There were no shooting down of allied aircraft (among other reasons because the alarm sounds so late that did not allow the B-24 to be "hunted"), but again the bombing of Sofia was not as massive as could be expected from such a formidable formation of bombers. The result was four bombers and five fighters damaged, but without any shot down over Bulgaria (although one fighter was reported as missing in the return to its airbase).

Only 8 days later, motivated by the lack of coordination of the various units in the air and antiaircraft, an exercise was carried out with aircraft belonging to 2/6 and 3/6 to about 8,000 meters height. It was also able to reinforce some up to 1,200 meters of aerodrome runways, to allow its use despite the harsh winter weather.

Finally the whole 2/6 was redeployed in Vrazhdebna airbase to facilitate the defensive tasks in the next attacks of the enemy.

20 December 1943

But what happened on 10 December was nothing more than a small presentation of how hard it would be to face the Americans in the Bulgarian skies and was also a demonstration that with proper organization (as they had exercised only two days before) and warned at the right time, the defense of Bulgarian skies could be more effective. According to Neulen and Nedialkov, another new mission aimed at bombing Sofia departed with at least 50–70 B-24 (Bulgarian sources speak of "Flying Fortresses" whenever they faced four-engined bombers, despite the incorrect terminology since such a designation corresponded to the B -17) escorted by at least 60 P-38. The B-24s were possibly deployed in three "V shape" formations on several steps in a long column and under cover of their escort fighters burst into Bulgarian territory, apparently in the direction of Ploiesti (although it was only a trick to confound the defenders).

Faced with this situation there was a rapid Bulgarian reaction, sending at 12.30 p.m. (12.20–12.35 according to Nedialkov) into the skies 24 D.520 from 2/6 (based in Vrazdebna) and 16 Bf.109G2 from 3/6 (from Bozhuriste) with the mission to intercept them before they arrived at Sofia (according to Stoyanov only 36 aircraft took off towards the Americans), both formations being at about 7,000 meters high, proceeding to form over Mount Vitosha. This joint action performed by fighters of German and French origin was the first time that was carried out and the results obtained were very interesting.

The first Allied wave they spotted consisted of 20 B-24s and 15 P-38s, and over this formation they unleashed their attack. Bulgarian fighters fought the Americans deployed in squadrons made up of four aircraft at 6,000 m height. The purpose of Bf.109G2 planes was to engage the P-38 fighters, whereas the D.520 should do the same with the bombers, with the main purpose of dissuading them from dropping their bombs on the city by forcing them to release them before arriving at their target. For this, the D.520 should not waste time in the combat against fighters, and making good use of their armament had to obtain the desired results against the bombers who came down from the south. The reality of the fighting led to greater confusion in the skies and the clashes of the D.520 and Bf.109 were against both fighters and bombers. The result of these first confrontations was only several American aircraft damaged, but the morale of the Bulgarian pilots rose thanks to the suitable organization that demonstrated in this occasion.

A second US aircraft group was approaching Sofia, so before entering the area of influence of the antiaircraft, they were attacked by Bulgarian fighters. The confrontation was brutal, so that the B-24s were made to drop the bombs before reaching their target. Most of the shot down planes were due to the group of Bf.109 from 3/6. Of all pilots it is fitting to point out Lieutenant Dimitar Spisarevski who managed to shoot down a B-24 bomber by ramming it intentionally with his aircraft, attacking it from below and behind (moments before in the same action he had managed to shoot down another B-24 with the guns of his plane). The Americans saw clearly that, although scarce, the Bulgarian fighters would not make it easy.

For their part the 2/6 claimed two shot down, a B-24 by Lieutenant Marinopolski from 652nd Yato and a P-38 by Lieutenant Nedelcho Bonchev. A total of 10-12 victories (3 B-24 and 7-9 P-38) were claimed in the clash, resulting in at least 5 B-24 ostensibly damaged, for the loss of two Bf.109G2 (with consequent loss of two pilots, among them the brave Spisarevski), another destroyed when landing (although the pilot was saved) and two others that returned to their base very damaged. And as a final result of the Allied mission, the bombers managed to drop 67,500 kg of bombs over the Bulgarian capital, achieving their objective.

As a curious fact, Spisarevski due to problems with the engine of his airplane could not take off at first, having to do so in a reserve plane with a certain delay of time with respect to his comrades. He was going to the first air combat, escaped from two escort fighters to go to a formation of 16 B-24, where he encountered his final fate leaving his dead body and wrecked plane in the town of Pasarel, close to Sofia.

4 January 1944

One hundred enemy planes (fighters and bombers) attacked at night and in thick fog, the city of Sofia without the antiaircraft or the fighters being able to do anything to prevent it. According to Nedialkov sources, only 15 aircraft from 1/6 commanded by Captain Rusev tried to attack them, but with no result. For their part, the Americans managed to bomb and carry out attacks with their fighters on the strategic objective of Dupnica, besides bombing in "blind" conditions due to the fog, locations like Rebrovo, Smoge or Carevec.

The night activities of the Bulgarian defense were practically non-existent and in this day it was clearly demonstrated.

10 January 1944

A formation consisting of about 220 B-17 escorted by about 110 P-38 (according to Nedialkov, 140 B-17, 40 B-24 and 100 P-38) was again directed towards Sofia to release its deadly load of bombs. To face them again 2/6 and 3/6 men, who on this occasion would not be able to stop the attack, being a fateful day for Sofia that was sown with death and destruction. 32 D.520 from 2/6 according Alexandrov based on colonel Petrov memories (23 according to Nedialkov, which seems more plausible) and 16 Bf.109 of 3/6 together with 30 Bf.109 German from I./JG 5 would be the defense forces of Sofia (K. Alexandrov says about this matter that in 2/6, D.520 began to be replaced by new Bf.109 so possibly some of the 2/6 aircraft were Bf.109).

The Bulgarian pilots, located at about 7,000 meters high, again tried to separate the escort fighters from the bombers, a fact that was at first achieved, leaving the Bf.109 especially dedicated to the escorts and the D.520 to the bombers (where their powerful cannon would play an important role). The 2/6 fighters when they located the first group of American bombers in their same direction, opted for a frontal attack against them, that got them to drop their bombs away from the target and to turn aside from its route; but it was only the first group of attackers. The problem was in the large number of American aircraft that saturated the Bulgarian defensive forces, meaning that the D.520 had to attack the bombers but also had to be embroiled in combat with the fighters; battles that were distributed over the skies near Sofia for at least 20 minutes. The end result was the indiscriminate bombing of the capital by the B-17 that had been left free from attack by the Bulgarian fighters; as well as a D.520 shot down, the one piloted by sergeant Atanas Krastev who was dead, and the forced landing of Lieutenant Natsev after facing in combat to 6 P-38. The D.520 acting on the much reduced formation presented by the bombers already fleeing to their bases pursued them as far as the locality of Bitolia (nowadays Bitola in south-west Macedonia). On the Bulgarian side, 4 B-17 (six according to Nedialkov) and 3 P-38 were claimed as shot down, as well as 3 B-17 damaged and at least 8 P-38 damaged.

According to some veterans' testimonies, some 4/6 aircraft that were forming in Karlovo during those days also tried to participate in the combat; although there is no certainty about it.

As a curious fact that Nedialkov reports, a German fighter Group composed of young pilots (their previous destination was Norway) with Bf.109G2 and G6 armed with two 20mm cannons in the wings and 210mm rockets had been fitted days before this bombing was at Vrazhdebna airfield. Their intervention in the fighting was disappointing, since of 25 aircraft that took off, five were shot down by the escort fighters (what did not allow them to get within the range of fire of the bombers) and only six were able to land at their departure aerodrome, dispersing the survivors across the area (in Sofia, Karlovo or Orhanie).

After the day bombing, that same night was followed by a night bombing, performed by 44 RAF Wellington bombers (and some Mosquitoes according to Nedialkov) from 21:50 to 23:35 completed a new night action over the capital. Despite the response of the antiaircraft gun (the fighters could not operate at night), it was not possible to shoot down any enemy aircraft.

The destruction of the capital was such that the downtown area was practically destroyed and the city could hardly be considered as such because of the unfortunate state in which the bombings left it.

After this attack, the following one also were nocturnal, the reason why the activity of the Bulgarian fighter forces was practically nill due to their impossibility to act at night. The only possibility of response to the night raiders were the salvoes fired by the guns, but also with little precision.

24 January 1944

A formation about 400 aircraft (bombers and escort fighters) was heading for Sofia in a thick fog. Because of this, many had to choose secondary targets by not being able to bomb the capital with precision.

According to Nedialkov report, some of the aircraft were intercepted by two German squadrons from Nis, which succeeded in destroying two bombers and two fighters between Sofia and Skopje. Forty B-17 that were going to Vraca were able to fulfill their task without problems, since 14 D.520 belonging to 1/6 did not manage to intercept them.

30 March 44

During March there had been a series of changes in the air war in Bulgaria. On the one hand, the two German fighter Groups based at Nis and Skopje were called upon to participate in the defense of the Reich. This resulted that in the Balkans Theater of Operations, the number of aircraft for its defense would not exceed 60 aircraft.

On the plus side, a Night Fighter Squadron consisting of nine Bf.109G6 was established. Although as we can suppose their number and the moment in which they appeared, motivated their practically nill effectiveness.

All this situation left again the 6th Polk as the only Bulgarian air defense weapon. 1/6 from its Karlovo base would give protection to the area of Plovdiv, Stara Zagora and Kanzalak; while 4/6 would be based in Asen (both units had at the end of March 28 operational planes). The remaining 3/6 in Bozhurishte (with 20 operational planes on the same dates) and 2/6 in Vrazhdebna (with 35 aircraft). And this was virtually all that the Bulgarian air defense could put into the air if necessary.

And that need would come soon, since after the bombings that took place during March, 16, 18, 24 or 29 (in nocturnal actions and therefore with no response from the BAF), March 30 would be the most intense that the Bulgarian fighter pilots had to live though, motivated by the biggest incursion up to that point by the American air forces. 114 B-17 and 253 B-24 of the 15th Air Force escorted by not less than 150 P-38 (223 according Nedialkov) deployed in four waves that returned to try to finish the Bulgarian opposition against their enemies. For this occasion 28 D.520 from 1/6 and 4/6 took off at 9:30, 20 Bf.109G from 3/6 at 9:35 and finally 2/6 aircraft at 9:50 (the cause of the delay was the bombing that had struck the Vrazhdebna airbase). The planes belonging to 2/6 were 6 D.520 from 662nd squadron and 19 Bf.109G from 642nd and 652nd Yatos. 4 Avia B-135 from Fighter School took part in the battle because of the great number of enemies, so they were called to contribute in the defense. In spite of the brave defenders, the bombers were mainly able to drop their bombs in their objectives.

The first to contact and fight the enemy were the Messerschmitts from 3/6 that detected the bomber formation at 6,000 meters with their fighter escort flying over them at 8,200 meters. Specifically those of the 692nd Yato first, then those from 672nd Yato. Later with the arrival of 682nd Yato, it became a violent battle with a multitude of individual battles over Sofia and to the west of the city, in which the Bulgarians forced many bombers to release their load of bombs prematurely.

Lieutenant Bogdanov from 2/6 directed his planes to chase the bombers, which they did for almost 100 km until contacting them.

The result of the action of 1/6, 2/6 and 3/6 aircraft was: 1/6 managed to shoot down two P-38 (by Lieutenants Schischkov and Terziev) and a B-17 (by Lieutenant Bogdanov); 2/6 shot down a P-38 (second Lieutenant Jordanov) and two bombers; for their part 3/6 shot down 5 bombers and one escort fighter. There may have been some more shot down but the complexity of knowing with even a minimum accuracy what happened during those few minutes in the skies around Sofia together with the confusion of many of the stories and narrations of the actions taken later, only allow us to get an idea of the results of that day.

In the area of casualties, they lost 1 Bf.109 from 3/6 and 4-5 D.520 from 1/6, in these last ones the pilots Jordan Kubadinow and Ivan Bojadschijev perished, as well as Ivan Pasow that was gravely injured.

We left to the end on this sad day, the memorable action in combat of four of the Fighter School's B-135 aircraft.

We have to remind ourselves that the Bulgarian B-135 was initially intended to be used by fighter units, but their continuous engine problems and their poor flight characteristics compared to modern fighters of the time relegated them to training functions. Perhaps the only noteworthy fact about this aircraft was its intended weaponry consisted of a 20 mm cannon and two 7.92 mm machine guns, but in fact these aircraft, as we mentioned, did not have the cannon installed, so that its fire potential was decreased noticeably. B-135 were already long used to fulfill their tasks of training, but on March 30, were allowed for once to fulfill the mission for which in distant 1938 had been created.

But with much more effective aircraft, why did they use these outdated fighters, now in instructive tasks? The reason was the need for the situation as we can now appreciate. The immense tide of American aircraft approaching Sofia that day to release its deadly cargo was made up of four waves of bombers (B-24 and B-17) with their accompanying P-38 and P-51 escorts. The first three waves were "received" by the Bulgarian fighter units, but the fourth caught the air defenses completely by surprise. When detecting this fourth wave consisting of about 30-35 (60-70 according to Boshniakov) bombers approaching from the north, the fighters were deployed in the following way:

- 3/6 planes were in Bozhurishte refueling and reloading ammunition. On receiving the news about the 4th wave, they managed to take off but before reaching the appropriate height the bombers had already dropped their bombs and were out of reach in the southwest direction (as did the four waves after bombing Sofia).
- at 11:05 am fighters from 2/6 (when they detected the bombers of that wave) were at the aerodrome of Vrazdebna refueling. They could not even take off to try to intercept.
- 1/6 fighters were in Karlovo, too far away from Sofia to participate in the events.

Faced with this situation of helplessness in Bulgarian airspace, we find that the only aircraft available for confrontation with the US bombers were four B-135 piloted by instructors at the School of Fighters. According to Bily based on colonel Velichkov memories and Boshniakov, these took off under the command of Captain Krastyo Atanasov to try to put them in a position of attack to the bombers that reentered Bulgarian airspace after the bombing. The other pilots were Ferdinandov, Manolev and Kolev.

The briefing for the attack must have been exquisite, since the old Avia fighter would only allow one attack on such a formidable air fleet. And in spite of being able to do it, the poor armament that carried the B-135 did not under any way guarantee the possibility of inflicting serious damage on the bombers.

Once he had seen the B-24, Atanasov supported by Lieutenant Yordan Ferdinandov fired at a bomber that they managed to shoot down (some other source reports that the four B-135 acted in the attack on that bomber, although it is more debatable). The plane that they shot down could have been a B-17F from 301st BG that crashed in the area of Tran and Breznik (already in Yugoslav lands), being the unique victory of this airplane in combat in its history. Although there will always be doubts as to whether the B-135 really caused this destruction.

B-135s subjected to both bomber fire and their own antiaircraft artillery attempted to attack the Americans again, but they were at the limit of their range of action to be able to return to some base; so Manolev landed at Dolna Mitropoliya base at 11:30 with the last drops of his fuel, while two other B-135s (Atanasov and Ferdinandov) landed at Bozhurishte, at that time the 3/6 base.

According to Atanasov, B-135 from School tried to intercept the enemy bombers on other occasions, that did not happen again, very possibly for the good of the Bulgarian pilots of this model of airplane.

As a final note to the activities of this remarkable day, the German aircraft that were still based in Nis, could not participate in the fighting due to the impossibility of taking off due to the poor conditions in which they had their runway.

4 April 1944

This month there was a new challenge for Bulgarian pilots trying to defend their skies, so they should be prepared for future combats. On 4 April for the first time, and before the arrival of a new formation of enemy bombers, the planes of the four Orlyaks took off simultaneously: 28 D.520 from 1/6, 23 Bf.109G and 6 D.520 from 2/6, 24 Bf.109G from the 3/6 and 12 D.520 from 4/6. According to Nedialkov only 3/6 aircraft located a formation of B-24 bombers without escort, obtaining only one enemy plane shot down by Petrov, besides they caused serious damage to other planes.

5 April 1944

Without waiting any longer and determined to finish the Bulgarian resistance in the skies, according to Alexandrov and Belcarz, some 600 bombers escorted by no less than 200 P-38 fighters headed for Bucharest through Bulgarian airspace, against which D520 from 2/6 and 3/6 were called to action. In this mission they managed to shoot down an enemy B-24 bomber by Veselin Tersiev, as well as to damage two P-38s.

Remaining Days Of April 1944

The American pressure against Sofia did not cease, so on 17 April about 350 B-17 in four waves (B-24 distributed in eight waves according to Nedialkov), escorted by 100 P-38, P-47D and P-51B flying at 6,000-8,000 meters returned to smash the

Bulgarian resistance. This time no means were spared to defend their country from the B-17s, since the usual P-38 are joined by the two most powerful planes in the United States in Europe (P-47D and P-51B). According to Nedialkov source, again 3/6 and 2/6 planes took off once received the warning of the approach of the Americans (they received the warning quite late, since they only took off about 26 minutes before the attack occurred); led by Captain Bosniakov with 30 Bf.109 (16 from 2/6 and 14 from 3/6) and two D.520 (from 2/6), then five 1/6 D.520 from Karlovo joined the Bulgarian defenders. As is reasonable the short period of time to react that the pilots had would hardly allow them to reach combat positions. In addition the aircraft from Karlovo, about 150 km from the action zone, arrives half an hour after the formation of 2/6 and 3/6.

In spite of these difficulties, once the clash against the formidable American Air Force took place, the battles began again by 3/6 pilots and later by 2/6. Two B-17s were shot down (most likely) by Captain Bosniakov and by Lieutenant Kovatsev respectively (the first plane fell in the vicinity of Küstendil and the second one near Rapec). Also in this air clash there was a case similar to the one that Spisarevski carried out in December of the previous year, that is to say, ramming the bomber with his fighter (in this occasion the protagonist was Nedelko Bonchev that had more fortune since he survived to be able to parachute from the wreck of his plane). At least two other Flying Fortresses were damaged and forced to abandon their formation, although without being able to destroy them. In addition at least four more Flying Fortresses were damaged by the fire of the Bulgarian fighters.

As we have commented, in this combat the P-51 appeared in Bulgarian skies. This fact had great importance in this fight since the Bulgarian pilots confused them by their silhouette in the distance with Bf.109 (since they expected the twin engined P-38), the reason why they let them approach without being attacked. This allowed the P-51s to approach firing range and cause the shooting down of three aircraft (with the death of their pilots) and forcing a fourth fighter to make a forced landing with his pilot suffering major injuries. The final result of casualties amounted to 9 Bf.109 shot down (with six dead pilots), without any D.520 being shot down; on the other hand a P-51B was shot down. The 2/6 was the most damaged Orlyak as it lost six of its planes and two more were damaged.

The antiaircraft artillery for its part fulfilled excellently to hit nine more aircraft (of which some would not arrive at their bases), with about 3,000 projectiles fired against their enemies (with a gunner dead and ten wounded). As was usual in these attacks, there were also bombs for other locations such as Doupnitsa (Dupnica) or Vratsa that were damaged on this occasion.

The bombing carried out this day was the end of the total offensive against Sofia that the Allies maintained through nine daytime and eight night attacks, which they again and again pushed against the ropes the Bulgarian air defense system. Despite this, 39 enemy planes (2% of the total) were shot down and at least 20 were significantly damaged, but 14 Bulgarian aircraft were lost (4.9% of the total) and 13 aircraft damaged; which averaged one enemy shot down for every seven combat sortie. From then on, again Ploiesti would become the main target in the Balkans.

For its part the Bulgarian capital had been destroyed, with most of its monuments damaged, such as the Ivan Vazov National Theater, the National Library, the Baths, Bulgarian Academy of Sciences and the Museum of Natural History. The people of Sofia, who suffered the heaviest part of the bombing campaign, had more than 2,000 casualties wounded and dead, but Bulgaria nevertheless continued in the war alongside its ally Germany.

5 May 1944

After the fighting on April 17, 6th Polk was quite affected, which is the reason why a restructuring had to begin with its available aircraft. New pilots were required, for which the Fighter School provided them every three months with a fresh set of newly graduated pilots. Fortunately Bulgaria had ceased to be the target of the Allied bomber forces, so these trainings could be carried out.

This day was the one that appears to be the last victory in which D.520 fighters participated (not completely confirmed), its victim being a B-17 bomber (by this time, there were still about 44 D.520 in service). It was a victory shared by Captain Petrov piloting a D.520 (from 4/6) and Lieutenant Planinski (from 2/6). In that same skirmish, Lieutenant Kolev (2/6) managed to damage another bomber that with two damaged engines had to abandon its formation.

In spite of being the last victory in the air of the D.520, it emphasizes that at the beginning of May still 44 specimens were in flying condition, and that it would continue in active for several months more.

18 May 1944

The situation was so critical in 6th Polk that at the beginning of May 1/6 and 2/6 did not have any operatable planes, and 3/6 had only six Bf.109Gs. For this reason, the victories of the decreasing BAF were diminishing, but this day they were able to shoot down two enemy planes. According to Nedialkov, one of them was a B-24 belonging to a bomber formation that was shot down in the vicinity of Pristina after having two of its engines damaged. The pilots in this victory were Bonev and Dakov who shared the victory. The other bomber was shot down by Tonchev near Prokupen. The small Bulgarian formation was composed of two pairs of Bf.109G, one manned by Stoyanov and the other one by Bonev; not only the leader but also his partner took part in the victories because this situation of relative calm in the Bulgarian skies was used by the veteran pilots to teach novices to take part in combat because enemies in the air were never lacking.

11 June 1944

During the summer of 1944 endless interception missions would continue against US formations targeting both targets in Bulgaria and using their skies as a "highway" to reach the Romanian oil complex in Ploiesti. According to Nedialkov on June 12 and 28, Karlovo's aerodrome was bombed, losing about 80 aircraft of various types in the attacks.

According to Nedialkov in June 11 a formidable formation of 600 B-17 and B-24 escorted by 400 P-38H, P-47D and P-51B/D was heading back towards Romania. A group about 200 bombers with 40 escort fighters separated from the main group across central Bulgaria. Against them again the tenacious pilots of 3/6 with 17 Bf.109Gs took off towards them. Four of these planes had to return because they did not have an additional fuel tank and the other ones, after some unsuccessful fighting, had to land in Dolna Mitropolia. The four aircraft that were returned were intercepted by P-51. Podporuchik Ivan Bonev piloted one of the four Bf.109s and managed to shoot down one of the eight planes that attacked him (it fell in Sredna Gora), but was finally shot down although he managed to jump out. According to the reports (Neulen and Nedialkov), he was machine-gunned by the American pilots while descending in his parachute, his dead body falling in Ovchelpoci.

When the formation of bombers returned from Romania, again the Bulgarian aircraft attacked. In this case four Bf.109Gs from 3/6 that once loaded with weapons and fuel were ready to take off from Dolna Mitropolia base (we have to remember that in that airbase 13 of the planes landed that had taken off against the American formation) in addition to another Bf.109G2 piloted by an instructor of the Fighter School based in Dolna Mitropolia. This small formation succeeded in shooting down two US B-17 bombers on their return to Bulgarian airspace. The pilots who achieved the victories were Tzvetkov and Rozev (the first one fell near Vratza or Vraca and the second near Pernik).

12 June 1944

There was no waiting for the allied response to the strong defense proposed by the Bulgarian pilots whenever an enemy formation flew over its territory. For the Allies the decision was easy, to bomb the air base of Karlovo, where 1/6, 2/6 and 3/6 Orlyaks resided. Nedialkov reports that the attack had to be carried out at night, so the British would be in charge of carrying it out. About 60 bombers separated into three groups of 20, were responsible for razing the important Bulgarian base in 20 minutes. In this attack, eight aircraft were destroyed, another eight badly damaged, 30 men died and 72 were wounded.

23 June 1944

Another confrontation against new waves of bombers on the way to Rumania and the Bulgarian fighters led to the consequent shooting down of two of them. One was shot down by the ace Stoyan Stoyanov which fell near Skopje; the other shot down by Hristo Toshkov. Also two other aircraft were forced to leave their formation after being attacked and damaged by pilots Damev and Tonchev respectively. Again Nedialkov reports that the participants in this battle were 600 bombers and 200 US escort fighters on one side and 34 Bf.109Gs on 2/6 (16 aircraft) and 3/6 (18 aircraft led by Stoyan Stoyanov) on the other.

24 June 1944

Once again, the Allies in their attempt to strangle the resources of the Axis in Romania returned to the attack. On this occasion 200 aircraft were used, against which the Bulgarians could only oppose them with 23 aircraft in flying condition (they were the 14 Bf.109G of 3/6 under the command of Stoyan Stoyanov and 9 from 2/6). This was another great day for the BAF as they were able to shoot down up to four enemy bombers of a new formation of Americans in combat over Bulgarian territory. The first claim by them (a B-17) was made by three pilots who shared the victory (Stoyanov, Uzunov and Kiril Stoyanov), the plane falling near the town of Samokov. The second crashed between the villages of Negotyn and Krivolak and was also shared by three pilots (Petkov, Tzvetkov and Damev), also note the fact that they were 3/6 pilots in their second mission in the day against the bombers. The remaining two were individual victories, one by Zagorski (the enemy plane fell near Bogdan Peak) and Petrov (near Samokov). According to Nedialkov this last pilot, belonging to 2/6, had after the fight enormous difficulties to return to the base at Vrazhdebna because of the enormous fuel consumption that it had in the same.

As a downside, clashes with US aircraft (especially with escort P-38s) resulted in the loss of some Bf.109.

28 June 1944

Despite their continued attacks on Romania and Bulgaria, the Americans were not satisfied. The reason was that in the case of the Bulgarians, they were still a dangerous enemy over which the bomber formations had to fly. So they decided that a new punishment was necessary, so that on this date about 150 bombers and escort fighters were separated from a larger formation that was heading for Ploeisti (composed of about 800 heavy bombers and about 350 escort fighters). The route that this "small" formation followed was to the aerodrome of Karlovo and the military factory in Sopot. The factory did not receive major damage (the factory air defense shot down a bomber), but the airfield that housed all D.520s (62 on that date) in addition to other types of aircraft, was severely damaged. The antiaircraft defense on this occasion could do little, as they only reached up to about 3,500 meters height, while the bombers maintained at 5,000 meters height. The result, in addition to the hangars and other infrastructure that were damaged, totalled more than 70 aircraft destroyed, 25 dead and about fifty people injured.

Definitely with this great strike, Americans managed to restrain Bulgarian air defense activities. The measures were immediate, as the different air units dispersed to avoid similar situations. One of the measures was the transfer of the remnants of 1/6 to the Asen aerodrome, the 2/6 aircraft went to an airstrip in the town of Banya (next to Karlovo) and 3/6 would reside in Bozhurishte where it would protect the capital with its 13 Bf.109Gs in service at the end of June.

The shortages of aircraft were appreciated more and more, the reason why a decision that was in the mind of Bulgarian Air Force leaders came to reality. It was necessary to concentrate the air defense units, so it was in June when the 4/6 was deactivated and their aircraft were integrated into 1/6.

15 July 1944

Hristo Kostakiev after a confrontation against an enemy bomber, is credited to have harmed it although without being able to confirm if it was shot down or not. It really could not have shot down the plane since no wrecks were found in the combat zone.

22 July 1944

This day witnessed the joint activity of German, Bulgarian and Romanian aircraft, trying to hunt about 1,000 aircraft (half fighters and half bombers) that were in action by Americans from the 15th Air Force.

The result of the Bulgarian attacks led to two four-engine bombers being shot down this day. One that fell east of the town of Kraguevatz was shared by three pilots (Toplodolski, Kralichev and Somov). The other was shot down by Bochev and fell near Babushnitza. Another bomber was damaged after the attack of Tzvetkov, although it only left the formation.

10 August 1944

The previous day Captain Atanasov was appointed as chief of 3/6, and then in August 10 he participated in a new air clash against enemy planes. With its 15 available planes, it fought a formation of 20 Americans B-24 (coming from a new bombing of Ploeisti) leading its unit. Nine 2/6 aircraft took off to participate in the interception of the bombers, but failed to locate them.

During the air combats two enemy planes were shot down: a four engine that fell near Nyshka Barnya (shared between pilots Bochev and Atanasov); and another similar bomber that after being badly damaged by Konzov, finally crashed near Samokov. Also another bomber was badly damaged and forced to leave its formation by the action of Bochev and Petkovski.

17 August 1944

The Bulgarian fighters had to take off again against another formation of four-engined bombers, although they didn´t manage to shoot down any of them (some sources says that possibly one bomber was destroyed), but they managed to partially disorganize it. The bravery and courage of the pilots led them to damage at least 7 bombers in the Skopje area.

26 August 1944

This was the date of the last bombing over Bulgaria, during which there were many human casualties, the systematic destruction of BAF aerodromes and villages, and many combat aircraft were destroyed on the ground (as happened to the B.534 for example, that they were decimated in such bombardments). It was also the last action of the Bulgarian fighter formations on the Axis side.

According to Nedialkov, Neulen, Boshniakov and Mandjukov, the protagonists of this last Bulgarian effort to defend their airspace were 16 Bf.109Gs of 3/6 that located a group of B-17 accompanied by their escort fighters. The pilots belonging to 682th Yato started the action, protecting the other two Yatos. The actions that then took place showed the courage of the Bulgarian pilots in a minority against their opponents (as usually happened because of Allied air superiority). They knew that little harm could be inflicted on the Americans in what has come to be called "Symbolic Warfare", but it was their duty, even if their life were in risk.

Along the fighting, Stoyan Stoyanov again demonstrated his skill in attacking enemy planes, succeeding in bringing down a twin-engine fighter (a P-38) near Vratza. A four-engined bomber near Vladishki Han was subsequently shot down in a victory shared by three pilots (Atanasov, Bochev and Takov). These were the last air victories of Bulgarian fighters before the coup d'etat and consequent change of side by Bulgaria.

Evaluation of BAF Fighter Forces

Since Bulgaria joined the Axis, its fighter activity was mainly confined to defending Bulgarian airspace as well as repelling the numerous bombing formations that were directed towards Ploiesti, Sofia or any other Bulgarian town.

According to Boshniakov, the number of Allied raids to which they were subjected was 23,000, compared to those who went on an interception mission on 1,100 occasions. As a result the Bulgarian pilots took part in 760 aerial action (of 970 fighting departures those headed by the 3/6 were 550, followed by 2/6 -275-, then 1/6 -90- and finally 4/6 -52-) they shot down 56 enemy aircraft both fighters and bombers (at least 37 four-engined bombers and 16 P-38 and P-51 fighters). Talking about these victories, D.520 for example managed to shoot down at least 5 B-17, 2 B-24 and 4 P-38; being the most important scores were evidently for the Bf.109 that acted as spearhead of the Bulgarian fighters.

As seen in the works of Nedialkov and Neulen, the anti-aircraft artillery also played a role (albeit small), which managed to shoot down four heavy bombers. It should also be noted that it is necessary to include 70 bombers and 22 other fighters shot down and damaged, in this list. It is stated that at least 117 accidents occurred to Allied aircraft during the missions carried out on Bulgaria and in the "corridor" over Bulgarian territory that allowed them to access Romania both on the outward or return trips, where many aircraft were forced to make landings. One last fact, 329 aircraft pilots and crew were captured, being interned as prisoners of war in the Shoumen internment camp.

On the other hand, 23 pilots and 27 aircraft (20 Bf.109s and 7 D.520s) were lost and at least 30 other aircraft were damaged in combat or suffered accidents (two-thirds approximately corresponding to Bf.109s and one-third to D.520s). In addition, the Allies dropped thousands of tons of high explosives and incendiary bombs over Bulgaria (although evidently in greater numbers on their capital) and resulting between April 1941 and September 1944 in 1,828 dead and 2,372 wounded civilians.

All these figures allow us to see that despite the material used, the chronic shortage of aircraft and the Allied dominion of the Balkan skies, the response of the Bulgarian pilots to the Allied formations in their national territory can be described as very good. This certainly contributed to the high fighting spirit and moral of its pilots in defending its homeland. On the other hand, the high number of casualties in proportion to their air force were caused by several factors. Although it is necessary to emphasize one important fact, as it was the lack of organization as much as structural, operational and strategic of the BAF, as we have commented on some

occasion throughout the text. While it is true that the vicissitudes of the war determined changes in this aspect, that lack of organization was an inevitable problem
that they had to bear throughout the hostilities.

Bulgarian change of side

After the communist "coup d´état" of September 9, 1944, Bulgarian aviation until
that moment allied to the German side, then started to fight it. As a first step as
far as aviation is concerned, it would be integrated into the Soviet combat forces.
1/6, the only one still with D.520 in flying condition (in September 1, they had 32
D.520s, but only 15 or 16 were in operational state) was at its Vrazhdebna base.

According to Nedialkov, Neulen, Mandjukov and Boshniakov, despite this fact, the
activities of the Bulgarian fighter branch would be paralyzed, except in specific cases
of reconnaissance over enemy troops, to focus on tasks of escort and ground attack.
The BAF fighter branch was definitely about to disappear as such. In fact, between
September 9 and October 7, 1944, the BAF performed more than 1,200 combat sorties
against the Germans, but always in support of the ground offensive and under the
control of the 17th Soviet Air Force. But the maintenance Bulgarian-owned planes of
German origin became very difficult, because at that time Germany was the enemy.
Due to this situation Bulgarian combat activities finished on December 2 with the
liberation of the southern region of Serbia. From that moment and more evidently at
the beginning of 1945 the sovietization of the country took place, and in the Bulgarian
air force, it will be reflected in the disposal of almost all its existing aeronautic park
and the arrival of surpluses of Soviet aircraft that will begin to enter service in BAF.

As a summary of the activities of the Bulgarian fighter pilots during the so-called
Patriotic War we can discover that despite the brief duration of this war and the
difficulties in keeping their aircraft ready for flight, Bulgarian pilots would manage
to shoot down 25 German planes and lose 21 of its own pilots as much by the action of German fighters as of the anti-aircraft artillery.

September 1944

As soon as September 10 an air confrontation between six Bulgarian B.534 and
six German Bf.109s took place at low altitude. Although the altitude did not play at
all in favor of the German fighters, they succeeded in shooting down a B.534, shortly
after breaking contact with the Bulgarians, very fearful of combat at low altitude
and the more than acceptable maneuverability of the B.534 in those circumstances.

Escort and ground attack activities were increasing and also the casualties in the
BAF. On September 14, a D.520 was lost when it was shot down while escorting
1/5 bombers.

Another D.520, piloted by Sergeant Petrov, was shot down by German anti-aircraft artillery on September 28. The ground-attack missions that the Bulgarians had assumed made their planes relatively easy for anti-aircraft fire, since neither the were planes designed specifically for the ground attack nor their pilots properly trained in this regard, which as fighter pilots were trained to much higher flight levels.

November

From early November, Bulgarian fighters were being repositioned at air bases in inner Bulgaria, so for example 1/6 was sent to Bozhurishte. In spite of this, the last combat missions carried out by D.520 took place between the 17 and November 20; then these planes were reconditioned to serve as trainers for future pilots.

January 1945

This month began the "cleaning out" of the material from German origin or obtained through them. For example, 27 D.520s were still in service status, but only until 1947 when they were scrapped. In the same way it would happen with part of the personnel, that were subjected to ideological purges by the new communist regime of the country in which men like Colonel Valkov (commander of 6th Polk) or Captain Petrov (commander of 4th Orlyak) were put under summary trial and then executed. Evidently from that time, the pro-Axis period of Bulgaria is "erased" from History by the new Government and therefore the participation of the Bulgarians in the world conflict was virtually forgotten. Only in recent years with works like those of Hans W. Neulen, Dimitar Neldiakov, Stephan Boshniakov and Petko Mandjukov has been able to really know the importance of the BAF and the role it played in WWII both with and against Germans.

Principle fighters (according mr. Nedialkov source)

Name	Nickname	Number	Year of arrival	Origin	Armament	Engine
HeinkelHe.51 B (one crew biplane)	Sokol (Hawk)	12	1936	Germany	2 7.92 mm machine gun	BMW VI 500 HP
Arado Ar.65 (one man)	Orel (Eagle)	12	1937	Germany	2 7.92 mm machine gun	BMW VI 7.3 750 HP
PZL P.24 B (one man)	Yastreb (Hawk)	14	1937	Poland	4 7.92 mm machine gun + 50 kg bombs	Gnome-Rhône 14Kds 760 HP
PZL P.24 F (one man)	Yastreb (Hawk)	22	1939	Poland	2 20 mm cannon + 2 7.92 machine gun mm + 50 kg bombs	Gnome-Rhône 14N-07 970 HP
Avia B.534 IV series (one crew biplane)	Dogan (Hawk)	78 12	1939 1940	Czechoslovakia	4 7.92 mm machine gun + 120 kg bombs	Hispano-Suiza HS-12 Ydrs 750 HP
Messerschmitt Bf.109E-3a (one man)	Strela (Arrow)	10 9	1940 1941	Germany	2 cannon 20 mm + 2 7.92 mm machine gun	DB 601 1100 HP
Messerschmitt Bf.109G-2 y G-6 (one man)	Strela (Arrow)	46 99	1943 1944	Germany	2 20 mm cannon + 2 7.92 mm machine gun (G2) 2 20 mm cannon + 2 13 mm machine gun (G6)	DB 605 A 1475 HP (G2) DB 605 A 1475 HP (G6)
Dewoitine D.520 (one man)	----	96	1943-44	France	1 20 mm cannon + 4 7.92 mm machine gun	Hispano-Suiza 12Y 850 HP
Avia B.135 (one man)	----	12	1944	Czechoslovakia	2 7.92 mm machine gun	Avia (Hispano Suiza) 12Y 890 HP

CHAPTER IV

Bomber units

The Bulgarian Air Force always lacked a modern strategic and tactical Air Force branch, since the fleet of both medium bombers and light attack and light bombers never lived up to that of its allies either in composition or in number. It is true, as we have commented on several occasions that the mission of Bulgaria as an ally of the Axis would be limited to control of a limited area of the Balkan territory with no more offensive pretensions, so the forces of attack and bombing would have not have been necessary. Reality, as always, was ahead of Bulgarian planning, as it suffered continuous clashes against partisan units in Yugoslavia, Greece and even Bulgaria itself. A modern air force might very well have played a decisive role in ending partisan resistance. Let us see how the low level of activity that Bulgarian bombers developed as bombers and how they were employed as tactical attack planes.

According to Nedialkov and Neulen, the first medium bomber that Bulgaria owned in WWII was Dornier Do.11D known as "Prilep" (bat) that served from 1937 until 1940 in first line units, until being replaced by the more modern Do.17. The total of the Do.11 was 12 machines that were integrated in the same squadron to make more useful; 5th Orlyak (Air Regiment 5) based in Plovdiv. This plane was modern several years ago but at the time they were integrated into the BAF in the second half of the 30´s, they were completely obsolete planes and lacking in power and speed, since their 9 cylinder radial engines were not at all reliable, giving rise to many problems in their maintenance. In spite of this the Bulgarian aviators managed to keep them in flight and in operational service during those three years forming the spearhead of the Bulgarian medium bombers force. Subsequently these aircraft were used mainly in transport tasks.

As early as 1940 was when a modernization of the Bulgarian bombers actually occured, although not at the same level of quality as in the leading air forces of Europe. It was in this year, when the Bulgarians benefited from the results of the occupation of Bohemia and Moravia (the Czech part of Czechoslovakia) by Germany. Since then the important Czech aviation industry was put at the service of the interests of the Reich. And one of these interests would be to modernize and increase the air forces of the Bulgarian ally. The German Reich obtained as war booty a series of aircraft that could only raise the level of the existing aircraft park, despite its disparate military value. Among these were the excellent but already obsolete Avia B-71 (Czech copy of the Soviet SB2). The B-71, which the order of acquisition reached 32 units, served together with the obsolete models previously on hand.

Another airplane that, thanks to German war booty, increased the bombing forces, was the MB200 of French origin (although produced under license by the Czech company Aero), known as "Buchal" (Owl-eagle). This plane, designed as a very modern concept a few years before, had passed to be obsolete compared to the bombers that were seen in the skies of Europe in the second half of the decade of the 30´s. They were characterized because they had supports for pumps under the wings. In addition its reliability did not satisfy their crews, the reason why it was not especially wanted by them.

By the spring of 1940, the 5th Orlyak amalgamated both bombing and training aircraft at its Plovdiv base. The models they had ranged from the acceptable B-71, Ju.52 or Fw.58 to the obsolete Do.11 or MB200, reaching a total number of about 56 aircraft in service. So since early 1939 the functions of the MB-200 despite being integrated into a Bombing Orlyak, were completely secondary and relegated to training tasks.

But the definitive thrust to the ever-increasing strength of Bulgarian bombers was the arrival of Do.17 "Uragan" (hurricane) that would finally replace the Do.11 in their missions. Although it should be noted that the Bulgarian Do.17 had a double origin. On the one hand Bulgaria received from its German ally 11 Do.17 in its M1 (bombing) and P1 (reconnaissance) variants in 1940; while shortly afterwards it would receive 15 ex-Yugoslav Do.17 Kb1 (bombers). The origin of these aircraft is because the forces of the Axis conquered Yugoslavia and Greece in 1941, so they were captured and ended up in Bulgarian hands. In addition also were obtained spare parts of all type and engines for the aircraft. The Do.17 Kb1 were discovered at the Skopje aerodrome (Skopje, present day capital of Macedonia or FYROM), some of them being damaged and only two in working order. Thanks to the spare parts supplies available to the Bulgarians, they were transferred to Plovdiv, where they were repaired and incorporated into the air force within the bombing squadron.

The Do.17 Kb1 were not exactly the same as the Do.17 of German origin, although both allowed the Bulgarian air forces to raise the level of effectiveness of the same at least as far as bombers are concerned. The Do.17 Kb1 delivered and later built under license in Yugoslavia (about 70 units) were based on the Do.17 M but made as an export variant that was characterized by having Gnome-Rhône 14N radial engines, retaining its defensive power in Browning machine guns of 7.92 millimeters and a 20 millimeters Hispano-Suiza cannon. Whereas the twin engines Dornier Do.17P and Do.17M were very similar to each other, possessing 3 machine guns of 7.9 mm type 15 and engines BMW 132H Bramo Hirt 323 P 1050 HP radial in the case of the M; or the BMW 132 N of 875 HP in the model P.

During a long period of time during WWII, the Do.17 were the core of the bombing and reconnaissance force in Bulgaria, although evidently supported by an amalgam of other types of aircraft.

Later and still in 1941, the Do.17 were assigned to the 1./5. Bombardirovochen Orlyak (1st Squadron of the 5th Bomber Regiment), where they served alongside the B-71 "Zherav" (crane).

As Nedialkov and Neulen refer, after the Bulgarian occupation of the territories granted in Yugoslavia and Greece at the end of April 1941, movement of aircraft were made so that on June 26 9 Do.17Ms and 6 B-71s bomber planes were sent to the aerodrome of Badem Chiflik near to Greek Kavala. From there they were easily able to carry out maritime surveillance patrols and protection of the Axis convoys that cruised in the calm waters of the Aegean.

Already as early as late September and early October 1941, the B-71s had their first intervention in the armed conflict against Greek partisan units that had been raised against the Bulgarian yoke in Thrace. Three B-71s left their base at Plovdiv and bombed the city of Drama, located in Macedonia and under rebel control after a violent revolt. But the air war against the guerrillas was not the ideal for the use of this bomber, the reason why this was the first and only intervention of the same while Bulgaria fought on the side of the Axis.

In August 1943, Bulgaria received from Germany more Do.17 to increase its existing Do.17 stocks (possibly they were aircraft seized to Yugoslavia). It was a de-livery of 12 Do.17 M (according to some other source it was only six units more). The performance of the new bombers focused on the Bulgarian occupation areas in Yugoslavia and Greece mainly against the Chetniks and Yugoslav partisans during the period 1941–1944.

After the change of side of Bulgaria in September of the year 1944, the Bulgarians had 29 Dornier, distributed 20 in 1st Squadron of the 5th Regiment of Bombers; 5 in the 3rd Squadron of the 1st Regiment of Reconnaissance and the other 4 in reconnaissance functions. The Dornier in the bombing unit began their new military activity from the outset, since 9 September, 9 Do.17 M of the 1st Squadron of the 5th Regiment of Bombers together with 9 Ju.87 D5s of 1/2 Squadron Stuka acted in the Bitola (Macedonia) zone in support of the 15th Infantry Division (according to several sources like Wawrzynski or Nedialkov). Also the reconnaissance Dornier began their operations from the first moment thanks to its long reach beyond that offered in the course of their missions.

Again a joint operation of Ju.87 with the Do.17 M took place almost a month later (November 3), 13 Stukas and 10 Do.17 taking part attacking German infantry formations near the Macedonian capital, Skopje.

One of the last occasions in which the Do 17 M were seen in action was performing bombing missions on November 12, when supported by Ju.87 and B.534 and escorted by 9 D.520 fighters, they bombed German troops in the area of Kachanik (a few kilometers north of Skopje).

For their part, the 21 B-71s in the 2nd squadron of the 5th Bomber Regiment still in service in November 1944 were moved mid-month from Plovdiv to their new Vrazhdebna base (in Sofia), from where they would begin his new period of activity, now against their former German allies.

Now the missions did not develop into an enemy that suddenly appeared and disappeared and took advantage of all the topographical features of the Balkan lands like the Ppartisans, but against a German regular army that was in full flight to the north, seeking the territories of the Reich and Hungary to avoid being surrounded in Yugoslavia and Greece. According to Stapfer, the B-71 bomber continued to be faithful to its scarce utilization throughout the conflict, during this period they were not usually those chosen to bomb specific targets, but rather on targets of opportunity in free search that would arise in their missions over territory controlled by the Germans. This is the reason why their interventions are mainly related to bombing of German units moving north and mainly located on roads or railways and railway stations up to four times during the war days against Germany; where they managed to destroy a motorized column, two train stations and three German trains.

On November 18, three B-71s attacked a German train at the Vuchitran railway station, and four B-71s bombed the Zhitarica railway station a day later and returned without casualties.

The month of November, even with the Germans in full retreat, was very fruitful for the attack aviation and Bulgarian bombers. On November 20, a formation of B-71s again ravaged German formations transported by rail in the areas of Mitrovica and Rashka.

A fourth mission flown by the B-71 was the one that took place on November 21, in which they were escorted by US fighters (specifically 15 P-38 "Lightning" of the 15th Air Force) aimed at attacking German units integrated in a motorized column near of Kamenica. In the same action, the American fighters were used to make an attack on ground objectives in the next train station in Mitrovica. This occasion was the only one in which there was an attack with Bulgarian and American air forces collaborating.

According to Stapfer, the use of the B-71 did not continue due to the long distance that in a few days separated its base of operations from the front line, since the Germans had to hurry to arrive at areas controlled by the Reich or its Hungarian ally, where at least so far, they were not in danger of being isolated and captured by the enemy. At the beginning of September 1944, only 12 B-71 were in flying condition according to Nedialkov.

The interventions of the different models of airplane in the Bulgarian arsenal were abundant, taking into account that in little more than two months of action against the Germans, the Bulgarian aviation struck them with 362 combat sorties. In these ones, the Bulgarian pilots claimed as destroyed a great number of vehicles and several aircraft; although according to the German sources, these were not so high. On the Bulgarian side, according to several sources, 173 motor vehicles, 42 railway trucks, 7 armored vehicles and 10 aircraft were considered destroyed or severely damaged; for the loss of 32 of their own aircraft and a good number of pilots and crew.

Bulgaria, despite the last-minute change of side, was also forced to settle its accounts in the war, one of which was the restitution to Yugoslavia of four of Ex-Yugoslavian Do.17 (possibly received in 1943).

Principle bombers (according to mr. Nedialkov)

Name	Nickname	Number	Year of arrival	Origin	Armament	Engine
Dornier Do.11 (4-6 crew)	Prilep (Bat)	12	1937	Germany	3-5 7.92 mm machine gun + 600-1000 kg bombs	2 x Siemens-Halske Sh.22-B2 de 650 HP
Dornier Do.17 M (four crew)	Uragan (Hurricane)	10 (M) 12 (M)	1940 1943	Germany	3 7.92 mm machine gun + 1000 kg bombs	2 x Bramo 323A-1 1000 HP
Dornier Do.17 Kb1 (four crew)	Uragan (Hurricane)	11	1941	Yugoslavia	3 7.92 mm machine gun + 1000 kg bombs	2 x Gnome-Rhöne 14N1/2 980 HP
MB.200 (five crew)	Buchal (Owl-eagle)	12	1939	Czechoslovakia (built under French license)	3 7.5 mm machine gun + 1200 kg bombs	2 x Gnome-Rhöne 14Kirs 870 HP
Avia B.71 (three crew)	Jerab (Crane)	24 8	1939 1940	Czechoslovakia (Tupolev SB-2M-100 built under Soviet license)	4 7.62 mm machine gun + 600 kg bombs	2 x Hispano-Suiza 12-Ydrs 750 HP
Aero 304	Pelikan (Pelican)	1	1939	Czechoslovakia	3 7.92 mm machine gun + 300 kg bombs	2 x Walter Super Castor I-MR 460 HP

CHAPTER V

Attack Units

The main strike force at the beginning of hostilities in Europe were the PZL.43A aircraft of Polish origin which had been acquired in 1938-39, although Bulgarian interest in them existed from as early as March 1936. Its arrival suffered several delays mainly related to delays in the delivery of the motors of French origin that would carry the Bulgarian PZL.43. In the beginning, the first 12 aircraft received were integrated into the 2nd Wing Squadron (2. YatoObrazcow Orlyak). According to Nedialkov and Kopanski, after receiving more examples of the PZL.43 from Poland, these aircraft were assigned to three squadrons (each with 12 aircraft) belonging to the 1st Line Bombing Group (Lineen Orlyak). In this unit they served in the initial stages of the conflict and carryied out missions mainly over the Yugoslav and Greek territories occupied by Bulgaria, where Bulgaria´s enemies abounded during this period of time.

The wear on these aircraft, as well as the need to restructure the various units of the air force, led in 1942 to dividing these aircraft into two different units; on the one hand the 2nd Line Bombing Regiment (Lineen Polk), and on the other the 1st Regiment of Reconnaissance (1. Razuznawatelen Polk). In the first of these they served from March of 1942 until August of 1944; while in the second its service was during the same period.

Due to their qualities and to the enemies that Bulgaria faced, the PZL.43A was used primarily in anti-partisan missions in occupied Macedonia until 1944.

According to Kopanski and Nedialkov, after the change of side, the PZL.43A "Chaika" (seagull) were integrated in two new formations that would make reconnaissance missions on the Yugoslav territories in which the German units were retreating towards the north, leaving its function of attack ended by the obsolescence of this kind of plane. These units were the 113th Short Reconnaissance Squadron (113. Yato za blisko razuznavanye) which used 13 PZL.43As between August 1944 and the first months of 1945; and the 123rd Short Reconnaissance Squadron (123. Yato za blisko razuznavanye) served with 11 PZL.43As during the same period. But the usual wear and tear on aircraft, the shortage of spare parts and several accidents they suffered led them to be withdrawn from service in front-line units from September 1944 (taking their place in the units it served was the indigenous KB-11) and the definitive service as early as the summer of 1946 when they will be regrouped at Lovech aerodrome for later dismantling. KB-11, on the other hand, was not involved in any significant actions, as the front line was moving away from Bulgarian territory day by day.

The best ground attack aircraft owned by the Bulgarian aviation was Ju.87 "Shchuka" (dive bomber), despite their obsolescence that was demonstrated in the skies of Europe since 1940. The first planes arrived in August 1943 and consisted of 6 Ju.87 R2s and R4 (another 6 of them arrived in September). These aircraft were not in good condition of use, having previously belonged to units of the Luftwaffe that had already made the best of them. This was the reason why they had to be used preferably for the purpose of training and adaptation of the pilots to the new airplane; which does not exclude that they were to fit into an attack squad.

Subsequently, the reception of new units of the airplane continued, although in future the Bulgarians would receive aircraft of the D5 model, much more capable and in flying condition. Received in different batches, the first arrived on January 13 1944, the next 19 in May, and possibly eight more in the middle of the year 1944.

According Nedialkov, Neulen and Wawrzynski, these Ju.87 D5 were all distributed in three Yatos (with 9-15 aircraft) that formed the 1/2 Attack Squadron (1/2 Orlyak Shturmovi or Stuka). Simultaneously, there was the 2/2 Attack Squadron that had another model of aircraft, which was nothing more than the ex-B.534 fighter, which, outdated in its former mission, had now been converted into a ground attack aircraft (after the infamous August 1, 1943, where the B.534 had made clear its ineffectiveness as a fighter, it was decided to relegate them from that role to entrust them with this one within the 2nd Attack Regiment). Both squadrons, both B.534 and Ju.87 formed the 2nd Attack Regiment (2 Shturmovi Polk) under the command of Captain Karavanov in 1944.

The use of both squadrons consisted of harassing the partisans who were at large in vast regions of occupied Macedonia and Thrace, as well as in some areas of the interior of Bulgaria. In fact, the first combat mission of the Ju.87 was against the partisans who were hiding in the Sredna Gora area in a mountainous region of Bulgaria, as well as in Yugoslavia. The wear and tear was such that of the 19 B.534s that were available on August 30, 1944, only 10 were in flying condition. At least one B.534 was destroyed when it was participating in an intervention against the communist partisans and several others were lost in accidents of various types.

The other anti-partisan actions were maintained intermittently until the coup d'etat of September 9, 1944. As a curiosity, it is known that one of the Bulgarian Stukas managed to fly towards the German lines piloted by a German instructor, before the change of side of Bulgaria.

As a curiosity suffice it to remember also that there also came to be employed in anti-partisan missions, other models of airplane not specifically attack types like the Fw.58. This was due to the reinforcement of the BAF with Bulgarian Fw.58, both in its model B and in the C2 that with its internal capacity and versatility conferred to it a role of "errand boy" in the BAF.

Following the coup d'état, most of the Ju.87 D-5s were grouped in the 1/2 Stuka Squadron (1/2 Shtuka Orlyak), where for the first time during the conflict, these planes were used on missions in the front line (and not exclusively in anti-partisan missions). The aircraft used the region of Macedonia (still under their jurisdiction) as a base of operations to carry out multiple harassment sorties for the German troops in retreat, while supporting the advance of the 1st, 2nd and 4th Bulgarian Armies.

Their first intervention was very soon, as on September 9 they acted in support of 15th Infantry Division which was surrounded in the area of Bitola, 9 Ju.87 D5 from 1/2 Stuka Squadron and 9 Do.17 M from 1st Squadron from 5th Bomber Regiment. In total this day 35 combat missions were carried out, among which we can highlight strafing against enemy land forces carried out by fighters. We are talking about the action where three Bf.109 from 3/6 attacked Nish airfield where they managed to destroy six German bombers deployed there but they lost a plane that was shot down. We have to remember that after the change of side, most of the missions accomplished by Bulgarian planes (of every type) were ground attack against their former ally.

After the change of side, the actions carried out by 2/2 Orlyak Shturmovy (with Avia B.534) completed at least 71 missions with 140 combat sorties in the period between 9 September and 12 November) claiming a large share of the casualties suffered by the Germans, such as 4 battle tanks, 22 artillery pieces, 52 motor vehicles, 62 wagons, a military train and various stretches of the Yugoslav railway line (according to several sources as Kudlicka or Nedialkov). In addition, they allowed themselves to return in a certain way to their former fighter role, while serving as an escort to their companion Ju.87 from 1/2 Orlyak Shturmovy in their tasks of attack.

The day after the coup d´état, September 10, at 0640 hours, a group of 6 B.534 when carrying out a mission on the railway area in Verinsko, was intercepted by several German Bf-109G, that despite shooting down an Avia plane (whose pilot survived), gave up with the others because of the difficult to face the very maneuverable B.534 at very low level, where the Germans lost potential in their aircraft.

Five days later, on another 2/2 Orlyak Shturmovy ground-attack mission, a B.534 was shot down by anti-aircraft fire at Tzurkvitza, near Kjustendil, and also the pilot survived by parachuting out.

The same result took place with a B.534 that was hit by heavy German anti-aircraft fire; this action took place on September 18 in another Avia attack mission. Although in this case the aircraft was able to return to its lines and landed, after being repaired it returned to active service.

On 24 September, another Avia attack mission, again against German ground units concluded in another B.534 damaged by anti-aircraft fire, but not enough to not be able to return to its aerodrome at Vrazhdebna, where finally it was repaired and put into service again.

As we can see the deterioration and continuous attrition in the Orlyak Shturmovy 2/2 was dramatic, due in part to the obsolete plane (with its rather limited speed) and because it was not a plane conceived purely for ground attack actions, but fighter actions. It was clear that the spearhead of the Bulgarian ground force could be none other than Ju.87.

At this point in the conflict, now with the Soviets on their side, the BAF had to adhere to the orders given by them. So Bulgarian aircraft would collaborate extensively with the 17th Soviet Air Force that was in the north of Bulgaria, arriving in September of 1944 near its capital.

Many of the clashes against the enemy on the ground occurred on steep and mountainous terrain (such as those in the southern part of Bulgaria), where the Bulgarians (better connoisseurs of their country) were supposed to act more properly. In addition to flying on own soil, they also acted as discussed, in Serbia and Macedonia. This entailed an added risk to that of the Germans themselves which was the danger of friendly fire. The Bulgarian aircraft were mostly of German origin and therefore similar in appearance to those employed by the Germans, so that they tried to delimit the areas of action of Russians and Bulgarians to avoid confrontations between them.

The next important action of Ju.87 took place on 5 October on the German positions in Belo (south-west of Bulgaria). As this action existed many during the so-called "Homeland War" in support of the various Bulgarian ground force units against the Germans until the end of November 1944. During the period from 9 September to 8 October, at least two Ju.87 were lost to German anti-aircraft guns and the Luftwaffe; although in the later days of the war the casualties in Bulgarian aviation would increase.

A new attack against German ground troops carried out by Stukas took place on 3 November in Skopje-Kachanik and Beley-Skopje (in Macedonia), 13 Stukas and 10 Do.17 M on a German column of troops fleeing. In this action the Luftwaffe made its appearance by means of Fw.190 from IISG 10 that at least managed to shoot a Ju.87. On the German side, ground troops suffered heavy casualties in the face of such an attack on German planes.

It is necessary to wait 9 more days for a new joint action between Ju.87 and Do.17 M, although in this case a new "guest" appeared, that was B.534 that was still active, now against the Germans. The mission consisted of the bombing of German troops in the area of Kachanik and took part in it the aforementioned bombing and attacks, escorted by 9 D.520 fighters. The results were good, since they fulfilled the objective of the mission without suffering any casualties.

As curiosity, it is known that one of the Bulgarian Stukas managed to fly towards the German lines piloted by a German instructor, before the change of side of Bulgaria.

After the conclusion of the fighting in Yugoslavia, the 1st Bulgarian Army was included in the 3rd Ukrainian Front that left in the direction of Austria from Yugoslavia and Hungary. The front line was very far from Bulgarian territory, the BAF did not have the capacity to follow the 1st Bulgarian Army that was under the "protection" of the 17th Soviet Army Air. The only remaining support to its compatriots was two Fi.156s and a Bf.108. Taking advantage of this situation, the Air Army underwent important changes in the command and structural; General Manchev headed it in January 1945, and in March of that same year began to receive Soviet aircraft that practically finished the presence of other aircraft in the Bulgarian aircraft park. Out of the total of 52 Ju.87s received by the Bulgarians, only 20 managed to survive the war (in January 1945, the B.534 ready for flight was no more than half a dozen), but only to be removed from active service during the same year 1945, due to the arrival of the "new" Soviet material.

Principle attack aircraft (according mr. Nedialkov source)

Name and crew	Nickname	Number	Year of arrival	Origin	Armament	Engine
PZL P.43 y 43A (three crew)	Chayka (seagull)	12 (43) 36 (43A) 2 (43A)	1938 1939 1941	Poland	4 7.92 mm machine gun + 600 kg bombs	Gnome-Rhone 14N-01 (43) 900-930 HP. Gnome-Rhone 14K (43A) 950-1.020 HP
Junkers Ju.87R2 y R4 (two crew)	Shchuka (Dive bomber)	12	1943	Germany	3 7.92 mm machine gun + 500 kg bombs	Jumo 211 1420 HP
Junkers Ju.87D-5 (two crew)	Shchuka	40	1944	Germany	3 7.92 mm machine gun + 1800 kg bombs	Jumo 211 J-1 1420 HP
DAR 10 A y F (two crew)	Bekas (Aggressor)	2 (proto-types)	1941 (A) 1945 (F)	Bulgaria	4 machine guns + 500 kg bombs (A) 2 cannons + 4 machine gun + 500 kg bombs (F)	Alfa Romeo 128 R.C.21 motor radial 9 cylinders 950 HP (A) Fiat A 74 R.C.38 radial 14 cylinders 870 HP (F)

CHAPTER VI

Reconnaisance and Liaison Units

Air reconnaissance tasks are vital for a country at war as it allows the acquisition of adequate information to make one or other decision at both tactical and strategic levels. But at the practical level, this branch of the BAF was displaced to second place behind fighter, bomber and attack branches, using lesser aircraft since the beginning of the war. Only the events that occurred demonstrated the need for more capable aircraft for this task that was twofold: short-range and long-range reconnaissance.

As Neulen and Nedialkov refer, at the beginning of WWII, one of the main reconnaissance aircraft available to the BAF was the German He.45. This model of airplane began its activity in 3rd Reconnaissance Orlyak (Razuznavatelen Orlyak), although immediately (in 1939) was replaced by the more capable and valuable Letov S-328. Once released from their reconnaissance missions, the surviving 11 He.45 were reused in the Training Orlyak (Instruktorskiego Orlyak), where they accumulated large number of flying hours.

According to Nedialkov and Vrany, Bulgaria received from the Germans and Czechs (from the latter, evidently by obligation), a batch of 62 Letov S-328 "Vrana" (raven). These would be used in reconnaissance tasks within the aforementioned 3rd Reconnaissance Orlyak based in Yambol and did not seem to act in ground attack roles (in spite of its capacity for it), planes like the B .534 being chosen for these anti-partisan missions. It is very important to consider that the missions against the partisans required good prior management of information collection that was achieved in many cases thanks to the S-328.

The S-328's reconnaissance missions lasted throughout the war, also participating in reconnaissance missions on Black Sea waters, although this issue will be discussed in the section on anti-ship units.

During one of these reconnaissance missions in 1944, there are reports that a Soviet Bell P-39 managed to shoot down two S-328s in the same action. True or not, it is clear that the capabilities of the Bulgarian S-328 against any Soviet fighter were minimal.

The utilization of the S-328 in reconnaissance tasks both on land and over the Black Sea, led to a rapid decrease in the number of operational aircraft that by August 30, 1944, led the 1st Reconnaissance Orlyak to have only 6 aircraft in flying condition.

Another aircraft used in reconnaissance missions was the KB-6 "Papagal" (parrot), of which 24 examples were obtained from the Kaproni-Bulgarski in 1941. These aircraft were only a Bulgarian version with the local license of the Italian Caproni Ca.309. Among the main modifications of the Bulgarian version were its redesigned tail, the use of Argus As.10C engines (instead of the original Alfa Romeo 115-II) and modifications to the nose of the airplane. It was also known as KB-309 because of its origin in the aforementioned Italian aircraft.

Its use was not only reconnaissance tasks but thanks to its versatility (despite not emphasizing anything in particular) was used as a transport or even as a light bomber; although in any case in a temporary manner and always motivated by the operational interests of the BAF. Their history in the BAF ends in 1946, when they were at last retired from active service.

Again a demonstration of the secondary character of the aerial reconnaissance branch was the incorporation to tasks of short-range reconnaissance of the obsolete and quite battered PZL.43 as the air force ranks were increasing with the new Ju.87 since March 1942 and being integrated in the 1st Reconnaissance Polk (1. Razuznawatelen Polk).

While it is true that the arrival of any aircraft to the reconnaissance units, although outside these characteristics, was always welcomed. Reconnaissance tasks often required being under the scope of enemy small arms fire, so having a plane that offered a certain degree of protection against it could prove to be comforting for its pilots.

The nationally-built KB-11 would be the new aeroplane chosen to replace, as far as possible, both the S-328 and the PZL.43 in their short-range reconnaissance tasks (it would only be possible to remove the PZLs after the Bulgarian change of side), managing to have a high number of aircraft of this model the Reconnaissance Polk to which they were slowly incorporating from 1942 onwards; evidently coexisting with other models.

The use of the KB-11 would consist mainly of joint reconnaissance flights together with Wehrmacht ground forces and the Bulgarian Army in Serbia against Tito's partisan troops. In these actions they played a worthwhile role between 1943 and 1944.

But the best aircraft that would swell the ranks of air reconnaissance units in the BAF arsenal was yet to come. We have to wait until 1943 for a modern and efficient aircraft created specifically for this mission to arrive in Bulgaria. This was the Fw.189A2 of which 18 aircraft arrived which became the core of the reconnaissance units (the number of aircraft in service on September 1, 1944 was 14; after the coup d'état only 7 aircraft survived in 333rd and 5 in the 334th Yatos). Following the coup d'état and the subsequent restructuring of the BAF, these aircraft were

A sparsely dressed man poses in front of a Bulgarian Bf.109E. We can see a canvas covering the cockpit and the engine cowling to protect them from the heat and dust.
[Courtesy of Stephan Boshniakov]

During the period 1945-1950 the national markings used by BAF were a circle of white and red with a green line crossing it. Here we can see a Bf.109G bearing this markings in the side of the fuselage and under the wings. In the background another Bf.109 shows us better this markings.
[Courtesy of Stephan Boshniakov]

Arado Ar.196 A3 of the 161st Squadron in the Black Sea. Thanks to this airplane, Bulgaria could control the waters of the Black Sea more effectively. [Courtesy of ASISBIZ]

A BAF Avia B-71 after an emergency landing at the base at Plovdiv. Due to the change of side of Bulgaria during WW2, it was sometimes escorted by its "old" USAF enemies [Courtesy of ASISBIZ]

Another image of an Ar.196 A3 in dry dock during maintenance at the base of Chaika. Black Sea waters were safer for Axis ships when this plane was patrolling because its deterrent effect. [Courtesy of ASISBIZ]

Staff of the 161st Squadron pose proudly with one of their Ar.196 A3 at the base of Chaika. This superb seaplane flew in all European fronts were Axis air forces fighted.[Courtesy of ASISBIZ]

Crew and ground personnel pose at the base of Plovdiv before a B-71 bomber. At the beginning of September 1944, only 12 B-71 were in flight conditions.
[Courtesy of ASISBIZ]

Several Bulgarian Junkers Ju.87D-5 flying in formation during a mission. This plane although obsolete in the Europe skies was still an important foe against ground targets. [Courtesy of ASISBIZ]

The satisfied Bulgarian delegation returns to one of the hangars leaving behind the Fi.156. In spite of his great interest Bulgaria would only be able to incorporate into the BAF several copies of this superb airplane. [Courtesy of Georgi from Bibliotekata]

The twelve seaplanes Ar.196 that Bulgaria adquired in 1943 multiplied the capabilities of Bulgarian maritime surveillance units. They were called "Akula" by his new owners. [Courtesy of Georgi from Bibliotekata]

Several pilots and crews pose proudly close to an Ar.196 A3 seaplane where we can see the 161st Coastal Squadron badge. Thanks to this seaplane, the Bulgarian controlled Black Sea waters would be safer to Axis ships. [Courtesy of Georgi from Bibliotekata]

The 161st Coastal Squadron (Yato) of Seaplanes located on the Chaika canal (near Varna) was the home to the modern Ar.196. Here a little dog take a rest over the wing of an Ar.196 A3 while is looking the plane´s badge. [Courtesy of Georgi from Bibliotekata]

In this picture we can see several mechanics tuning an Ar.196. This seaplane played an important role controlling Bulgarian waters but when Bulgaria moved on to the Allied side the Ar.196 had little participation in the war conflict due to the northward withdrawal of Axis forces. [Courtesy of Georgi from Bibliotekata]

Side view of Ar.196 A3 number 3, out of the water. From Chaika canal, these modern seaplanes allowed Bulgaria better control of its territorial waters and deter Soviet ships and submarines. [Courtesy of Georgi from Bibliotekata]

Several Bulgarian pilots pose close to a battered D.520. The last victory in the air of the D.520 was on 5 May 1944; by this time there were still about 44 D.520 in service.
[Courtesy of Stephan Boshniakov]

One pilot pose quietly over the first Avia B-135 of a line of at least four planes. These aircrafts due to its obsolescence were not used as fighter but as trainers in the Fighter School in Dolna Mitropoliya. [Courtesy of Georgi from Bibliotekata]

A pilot poses for the camera before take off. We can see the St. Andrew´s Cross on the side of the fuselage and on the left wing, that was the BAF national insignia from 1941 to 1944. [Courtesy of Georgi from Bibliotekata]

A line of Avia B.534 close to their hangar. Although at the beginning this plane was considered as a fighter, at the end of the war only was used as an attack aircraft. On August 30, 1944 from 19 B.534s available, only 10 were in flight conditions. [Courtesy of Georgi from Bibliotekata]

An Avia B.534 "Dogan" (hawk) after a crash landing. The wear and tear on this kind of plane
was very high because it was used intensely from the beginning of the war.
[Courtesy of Georgi from Bibliotekata]

Side view of a brand new Avia B.534 showing the BAF Coat of arms used from 1937 to 1941. In 1939 the 2nd Fighter Orlyak based in Karlovo had about 60 Avia B.534 in four Fighter Yatos.
[Courtesy of Georgi from Bibliotekata]

Several military officers receive the pilot of an Avia B-135. We can appreciate the two blades propeller typical of this airplane. Bulgarian Avia B-135 didn´t have cannon but
2 7,92 mm machine guns.
[Courtesy of Georgi from Bibliotekata]

A pair of Arado Ar.96 from the more than 40 received from Germany in a grass airfield. This kind of plane was one of the main trainers in BAF, along with Caproni-Bulgara CB 5, DAR 9 and Focke Wulf Fw.44J. [Courtesy of Georgi from Bibliotekata]

Three pilot have a briefing before take off. Close to them is an advaced monoplane trainer. The training of new pilots became a very important task within the BAF.
[Courtesy of Georgi from Bibliotekata]

A S-328 "Vrana" flying over the Black Sea coast looking for Soviet ships and submarines. They were based in Safarovo and Balchik and although they were obsolete airplanes they did their best in antisubmarine and reconnaissance missions. [Courtesy of Fernando Salobral]

The twin engined Focke Wulf Fw.189A 2 "Oko" was one of the few modern kind of plane that Bulgaria had during WW2. Here we can see the crew entering in the cockpit helped by ground staff. [Courtesy of Georgi from Bibliotekata]

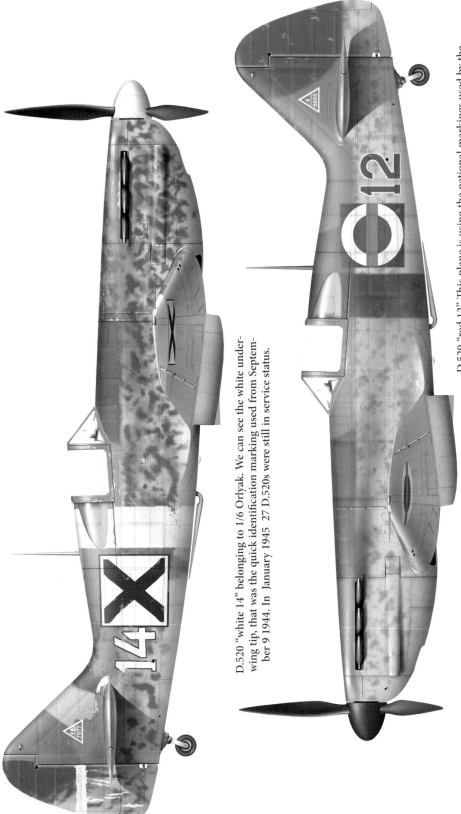

D.520 "white 14" belonging to 1/6 Orlyak. We can see the white under-wing tip, that was the quick identification marking used from September 9 1944. In January 1945 27 D.520s were still in service status.

D.520 "red 12" This plane is using the national markings used by the BAF during the period 1945-1950 which was a circle of white and red with a green line crossing it, that replaced the St. Andrew´s Cross. The previous Theater bands have been overpainted.

Painted by Arkadiusz Wróbel

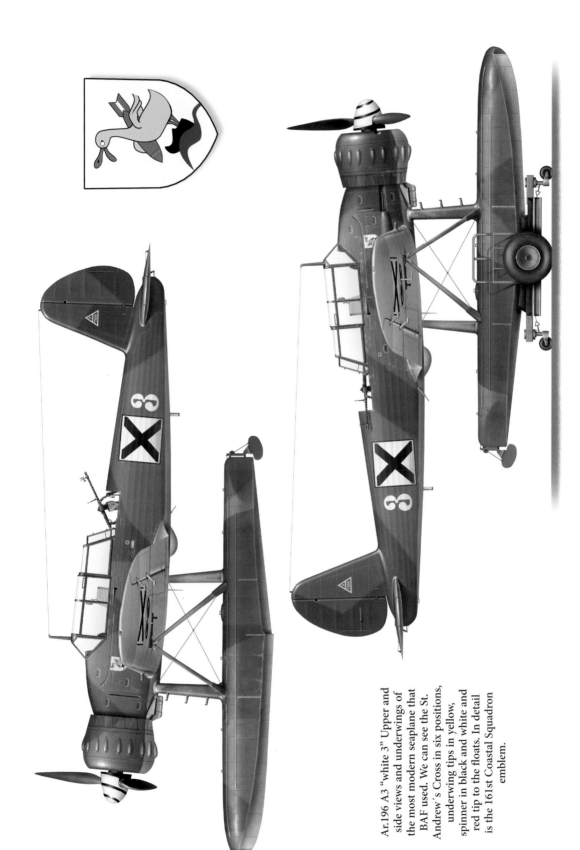

Ar.196 A3 "white 3" Upper and side views and underwings of the most modern seaplane that BAF used. We can see the St. Andrew´s Cross in six positions, underwing tips in yellow, spinner in black and white and red tip to the floats. In detail is the 161st Coastal Squadron emblem.

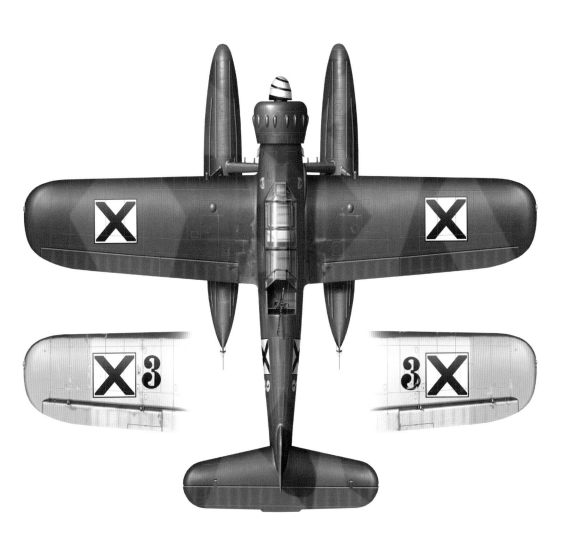

Ar.196 A3 "white 7" belonging
to 161st Coastal Squadron.
The seaplane bears the yellow
Theater band in the middle of
the fuselage as a Germany ally.
The total of the Ar.196 "Akula"
acquired by Bulgaria were 12
units, which were put into
service by June 1943.

Ar.196 A3 "white 5". This
seaplane bears the insignia used
by BAF from 1945 to 1950.
Bulgaria had in active service
only 8 "Akula" when moved on
to the Allied side. Since that
moment the Ar.196 had little
participation in the war conflict
due to the northward withdrawal
of Axis forces.

Painted by Arkadiusz Wróbel

integrated into the 333rd (with 8 planes) and 334th (with 6 planes) Yatos from 1/3 Orlyak based in Varba aerodrome, near the border with Serbia.

Their excellent flying characteristics, their good visibility and the cameras they carried, represented a great leap forward for aerial reconnaissance. This activity was a great help in coordinating ground troops and their subsequent tactical movements. Their missions were carried out throughout the country, with special attention to the theoretically most conflicted areas of the south and west.

After the change of side by Bulgaria of 1944, the Fw.189 from 1/3 Orlyak continued their reconnaissance missions, accompanied occasionally by ground attacks (a task that had not been necessary until that time when they were allies of Germany) and others that helped to guide artillery fire. As Nedialkov refers, these activities were always in support of the 1st and 4th Armies heading towards Skopie and Veles respectively (from their air base they accomplished missions against Germany over Serbia, Macedonia and Hungary). As a curiosity, another plane of the reconnaissance force, the KB-11 (grouped in the 1st and 2nd Yatos of Tactical Reconnaissance), did not see much use against its old German allies possibly due to its resemblance to the German Henschel Hs-126, which could lead to major confusions including "friendly fire". Despite this, they also participated in support of Bulgarian troops in Macedonia and Serbia.

Continuing with the Fw.189, they took part in a merger with their "brother" KB-11 from 1/4 Orlyak (based in Bozhuriste) in numerous reconnaissance missions on the German enemy in retreat. In the period between September 9 and October 7, 1944 (before the Bulgarian ground offensive), from more than 1.200 combat departures performed, about 350 were carried out by the 1/3 and 1/4 Orlyak aircraft.

From that date, on October 8, 1/3 Orlyak began with its tasks of light attacks on ground convoys of German vehicles immediately behind the front line. In particular, the Fw.189 managed to destroy up to 8 trucks and many other German vehicles in retreat, so that the bombs that these planes and machine guns (in a second place) caused much damage. As we can see, the role of these "pure" reconnaissance planes, began to change in order to get the most out of one of the few modern and really capable aircraft types of the whole BAF. It was necessary to wait until October 17 for another new type of mission to be carried out by the Fw.189, in this case planes from 333th Yato (1/3 Orlyak) acted as guides for artillery fire of the ground troops in the attack to the bastion of Strazhin; subsequently continuing its actions in the actions against Belgrade.

This brief period of fighting against Germany greatly diminished the number of Fw.189 available, since in addition to the enemy in front of them, it is also necessary to consider that these aircraft went from performing missions at high level (in reconnaissance) to carrying out attacks at ground level, so inevitably the result was more than predictable. But the Bulgarians had to pay that fee to their new allies. In spite of this, the actions of the Fw.189 in any of the roles in which they were used always were met with great success by these extraordinary aircraft and their pilots who had to be re-roled very well, as the war was advancing.

Another sample of Bulgaria's "payment" to the victors after the end of the war was the delivery of 30 KB-11 to Yugoslavia in 1947 as war reparations; where they would remain in service until 1958.

We have left to finish the text about reconnaissance units, the secondary aspect that these should cover: long-range reconnaissance. In this section it is necessary to agree that Bulgaria was not far behind, since with the acquisition of the Do.17P1 for long-range reconnaissance, they had equipment not modern, but quite adequate.

In 1944, prior to the coup d'etat, integrated into the 1st Reconnaissance Polk was the 73rd Yato of Long Range Reconnaissance constituted by Do.17P, with its main base in Sofia. Shortly after the change of side, these reconnaissance Do.17s were the only Do.17s Bulgarians that flew in actions against the Axis troops combining its main mission with others like observation and liaison.

In any air force, a small group of aircraft must meet the least known aspect of liaison units, observation for artillery and transport of commanders or messengers; what is called "liaison aircraft". In addition, their versatility allowed them to perform other missions such as reconnaissance, medical evacuation or transport, etc.

The aircraft used in these missions are always characterized by their good flying and observation qualities, as well as the ability to take off and land in very short distances even from improvised aerodromes or in poor conditions.

Although acquired in 1940, it was in 1941 when another advanced aircraft was incorporated into the liaison units, as was the case with Bf.108B1. Of these, 6 were acquired that were integrated in the Yuri Kurierskiego Yato (Liaison Yato) and would continue in service until the end of 1944 or beginning of 1945 (giving support to Bulgarian ground Forces against the Germans). These aircraft successfully fulfilled their task of linking the many Bulgarian units dispersed over Bulgarian territory.

The other airplane that fulfilled the same mission that the previous one was the excellent Fi.156C, of which in 1941 3 examples were acquired that also acted within liaison units; in particular in the FAB Headquarters Yato (according to Karnas, Bulgaria received 12 Fi.156 during summer 1943 and then 4 Fi.156 in the medevac version in January 1944). This excellent aircraft, ideal for the tasks of liaison, would have an active life similar to that of the Bf.108, becoming less important when Bulgaria went over to the Allied side and material of German origin was generally replaced by that of origin Soviet. At least one of the Fieseler aircraft was shot down by fire from German light weapons, killing two of its occupants.

Circumstantially other aircraft could be used in liaison missions, due to their suitable flying characteristics. Among them was Fw.58, which, as we have observed, was more than useful in various roles such as transport, training or light attack. In the situation of chronic shortage of aircraft of the BAF, some multipurpose aircraft gave good service being used indistinctly for some tasks or others according to the operational necessities of the moment; showing a clear example of which Fw.58 was.

Main aircrafts of reconnaissance, observation and liaison
(according Mr. Nedialkov source)

Name	Nickname	Number	Year of arrival	Origin	Armament	Engine
Heinkel He.45 (two crew biplane)	Shturkel (Stork)	12	1936	Germany	2 7.92 mm machine gun + 300 kg bombs	BMW VI-J32 750 HP
Fieseler Fi.156 Storch (two crew)	Drozd	3	1941	Germany	1 7.92 mm machine gun	Argus 240 HP
Focke Wulf Fw.189A 2 (three crew)	Oko (Eye)	18	1943	Germany	6 7.92 mm machine gun.	2 x Argus As410A-1V 465 HP
Letov-Smolik S.328 (two crew biplane)	Vrana (Crow)	62	1939	Czechoslovakia	4 7.92 mm machine gun + 500 kg bombs	Bristol Pegasus II.M-2 built by-Walters 650 HP
Messerschmitt Bf.108 B1 (two crew)	Lebed	6	1940	Germany	–	Argus 240 HP
Focke Wulf Fw.58 (up to 6 people)	Golob (Dove)	8	1937	Germany	2 ametrall de 7.9 mm + bombas (opcional)	2 x Argus As 10C 240 HP
Potez XV/XVII (two crew biplane)	–	2 (XV) 6 (XVII)	1924 1926	France	2 7.7 mm machine gun 300 kg bombs (XVII)	Lorraine-Dietrich 400 HP
KB-11, 11A (two crew)	Kvazimodo (11 Prototype) (Quasimodo) Fazan (11) (Pheasant) Fazan (11A)	1 (11 Prototype) 6 (11) 43 (11A)	1940 (11 Prototype) 1941 (11) 1942 (11A)	Bulgaria	–	Alfa Romeo 126 R.C.34 750 HP (11 Prototype and 11). Bristol Pegasus XXI 1,000 HP (11A)
Dornier Do.17 P (four crew)	Uragan (Hurricane)	18	1940	Germany	3 7.92 mm machine gun	2 BMW 132 N, 875 HP
Dornier Do.17 Ka1 (four crew)	Uragan (Hurricane)	4	1941	Yugoslavia	3 7.92 mm machine gun	2 x Gnome-Rhöne 14N1/2 980 HP

CHAPTER VII

Training Units

Since the mid-1930s, efforts were made to increase the few training aircraft available to the BAF. Due to the upsurge in acquisition of new aircraft from 1936, a good quantity of training aircraft was obtained to begin to restructure the training units for new pilots. The idea in mind was to create a capable and self-sufficient air force to train new pilots.

Another source of arrival of new training aircraft was motivated by this acquisition of new models of aircraft, since some types were becoming outdated in a very short time, like the Ar.65 or He.51 (previously fighters) or MB-200 (which went from bomber to bomber training plane).

Another plane that followed the same steps as the previous ones was the He.45, which went from acting in the 3rd Reconnaissance Orlyak, to increase in 1939 the ranks of the Training Orlyak. The number of these robust aircraft that transfered to training tasks was 11 units.

Nedialkov and Neulen refer that immediately before WWII, as we saw, the structure of the BAF contained the Training Yunker Orlyak (at Vrazhdebna aerodrome), a Training Orlyak (also based in Vrazhdebna in Sofia) and the Air School (based in Kazanluk), in addition to an integrated Training Yato within the 1st Line Orlyak (based at Bozhurishte), 2nd Fighter Orlyak (based in Karlovo), 3rd Reconnaissance Orlyak (based in Yambol) and 5th Bomber Orlyak (based in Plovdiv) to which the School of "Blind" Flight was attached. This fact demonstrates the importance that the high command of the BAF granted to the training of future pilots for the growing air force. In spite of which, we can consider that the BAF was always deficient in pilots, as well as modern machines during the greater part of the conflict.

The main aircraft used by these training units were Ar.65, He.51, Fw-56, B.534, B-122 in the case of advanced training, or He.45, Fw-44, KB 3, Bü.133, Ar.96, Fw.58, He.72, PWS-26 (two examples were obtained by two Polish pilots flying to Bulgaria in 1939 to avoid falling into German hands), DAR-8 or DAR- 9 or others of indigenous production like the KB-2. In addition to the aircraft that were retired from the front line, also used as advanced training aircraft were: PZL.43, MB-200, Ju.87R, etc. Other aircraft that were used had been quite obsolete since they were acquired in the 20´s.

As a matter of interest motivated by the structure of the BAF, it should be noted that eight Fw.58 were integrated in the 5th Bomber Polk (at the beginning of the WWII an Orlyak would become a Polk). Obviously the mission of these planes could not be one of bombing, but remember that this Polk was divided into two Orlyak, that in turn consisted of 5 Yatos, one of which was for instrument training and of flying in multi-engined planes (and is here where the twin engine Fw.58s played their role). Also with similar tasks were the venerable MB-200 bombers that due to their obsolescence were allocated to training, being also assigned to the "School of Bomber Training" existing at Vrazhdebna airport, in Sofia.

Although Ar.65 was used in a initial and brief period as a fighter, they were evidently old-fashioned almost immediately in BAF when new models of superior performance arrived. As the planes were in good condition, they were assigned to the mission of training and as an advanced trainer for the new batches of pilots that were emerging. The Ar.65 never got to be appreciated by its crew either during its activity like fighter or when it transferred to the role of training by its complicated flight characteristics. A similar situation to that of the Ar.65, the He.51 that had to pass from their fighter role to the trainer role.

The Ar.65s were placed in various training units, especially the Kazanluk base where the 1st and 2nd Aerial Training Schools were deployed. Right there in Kazanluk was the aircraft factory Bulgarski-Kaproni that saw the birth of various models of aircraft that would also be used as trainers such as KB2 UT.

Principle training planes (according mr. Nedialkov source)

Name	Nickname	Number	Year of arrival	Origin	Armament	Engine
Arado Ar.96 A (two crew)	Soyka	3	1941	Germany	–	Argus AS 410 478 HP
Arado Ar.96 B2 or DAR 9 (license built)	Soyka	42	1940	Bulgaria	–	Siemens 160 HP
Avia B.122 (one man biplane)	Osa	29	1939	Czechoslovakia	–	Avia RK 17 350 HP
Heinkel He.72 (two man biplane)	Karnacze (Canary)	6	1938	Germany	–	BMW Bramo 160 HP
Focke Wulf Fw.44J (two man biplane)	Vrabche (Sparrow)	42	1936	Germany	–	Siemens-Halske Sh 14 125 HP

Name	Nickname	Number	Year of arrival	Origin	Armament	Engine
Caproni-Bulgara CB 1 (two man biplane)	Peperuda (Butterfly)	7-10	1932	Bulgaria	–	1 Walter NZ radial 120 HP
Caproni-Bulgara CB 2 (two man biplane)	Chuchuliga (Skylark)	6	1936	Bulgaria	–	Walter Castor radial 240 HP
Caproni-Bulgara CB 2 UT (two man biplane)	Chuchuliga	7	1936	Bulgaria	–	1 BMW IVa inline 250 HP
Caproni-Bulgara CB 3 (two man biplane)	Chuchuliga I	20	1937	Bulgaria	–	Walter Castor II radial 340 HP
Caproni-Bulgara CB 4 (two man biplane)	Chuchuliga II	28	1938	Bulgaria	–	Wright Whirlwind R-975 E-2 220 HP
Caproni-Bulgara CB 5 (two man biplane)	Chuchuliga III	45	1939	Bulgaria	–	Walter Pollux II 450 HP
Caproni-Bulgara CB 309 or CB 6	Papagal (Parrot)	24	1941	Bulgaria	3 7.7 mm machine guns + 300 kg bombs	Argus As10C 2 x 240 HP
DAR 1 y 1A (two man biplane)	Peperuda	12(1) 8 (1A)	1926 1928	Bulgaria	–	Walter NZ 60 HP (1) Walter Vega 85 HP (1A)
DAR 2 (two man biplane)	Albatros CIII	26	1926	Bulgaria	–	Mercedes D.III 160 HP
DAR 3 (two man biplane)	Garvan (Crow)	6 (series 1) 6 (series 2) 12 (series 3)	1936 (series 1) 1937 (series 2) 1939 (series 3)	Bulgaria	–	Wright Cylone (serie 1) Alfa Romeo 126 RC 34 (series 2) Alfa Romeo 126 RC 34 (series 3)
DAR 4 (biplane, two crew and 4 passengers)	–	1 (prototype)	1930	Bulgaria	–	3 radial de 145 HP
DAR 5 (one man biplane)	Brambar (Beatle)	1 (Prototype)	1930	Bulgaria	–	220 HP
DAR 6 y 6A (two man biplane)	---	1 (prototype) and 1	1937 (6) 1938 (6A)	Bulgaria	–	Walter Mars 85 HP (6) Siemens Sh-14A 160 HP (6A)

Name	Nickname	Number	Year of arrival	Origin	Armament	Engine
DAR 8 (two man biplane)	Slavey (Mocking-bird)	13	1937	Bulgaria	–	Walter Major IV 130 HP
DAR 9 (two man)	Siniger (Mouse)	42	1940	Bulgaria	–	Siemens 160 HP
Bucker Bu.181 (two man)	Ljastovitza (Swallow)	12	1943	Germany	–	Hirtz XM 100 HP
CB=KB= Kapro-ni-Bulgarski= Caproni-Bulgara						

A B-24 Bomber from 376th USAAF Bomber Group bombing Sofia in April 1944. The Bulgarian capital was the target of USAF bombers several times. [From Public Domain]

Heavy Bomber B-24th from 44th USAAF Bomber Group bombing Ploiesti during Operation Tidal Wave in 1943. Bulgaria acted as a mere trip way for the bombers that had departed from Africa, then flew to Greece and Albania, crossing Bulgarian Macedonia and north-west Bulgaria and then toward Ploiesti. [From Public Domain]

Four USAAF P-51D, possibly the fiercest rival that BAF aircrafts found in the air. In spite of this, Bulgarian fighters did their best against P-51. [From Public Domain]

An USAF B-17 Heavy Bomber in Action. Another of the rivals of the Bulgarians in the air that was a very dangerous foe due to their superb defensive armament. [From Public Domain]

Another of the powerful rivals of the BAF, the medium bomber B-25. Medium and heavy bombers helped by fighters and fighter-bombers dominated Bulgarian skies without any possible and effective Bulgarian response. [From Public Domain]

BAF national insignia from 1945 to 1948.

BAF national insignia 1937 to 1941.

BAF national insignia from 1941 to 1944.

[From Public Domain]

One P-47N fighter bomber, perhaps one of the most difficult to shoot down in combat by Bulgarian planes. This plane was very dangerous for Axis as in the air combat as in ground attacks. [From Public Domain]

One of the two copies of the DAR 10 attack that never reached its serial production stage. One of the Bulgaria Air Force great hopes that never came true. We can see the St.Andrew´s cross in the fuselage.
[From Public Domain]

One of the first American rivals found by the Bulgarian pilots: P-38. Here four planes in flight in formation.
[From Public Domain]

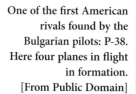

Imagen of the triple occupation of Greece by Germany, Italy and Bulgaria during 1941–1944.
[From Public Domain by Cplakidas]

Bulgaria had to to wait until 1943 for a modern and efficient aircraft created specifically for reconnaissance missions to arrive in Bulgaria: the Fw.189A2. In this picture we can see the badge that this kind of plane used, an eye (the same as the nick that the plane received).
[Courtesy of Georgi from Bibliotekata]

Only 18 units of the Fw.189A2 arrived to Bulgaria and they became the heart of the reconnaissance units. In this picture a Fw.189A2 is taxiing before the take off from its airfield.
[Courtesy of Georgi from Bibliotekata]

This idyllic picture where the pilot Popganchev reads a letter over the grass close to his Avia B.534 remind us to early 30´s, but this plane was used by BAF during al WW2. In spite of this, their pilots did their best in every mission with or against Germany.
[Courtesy of Stephan Boshniakov]

Four pilots pose proudly in front of a faultless Avia B.534. Bulgaria took the opportunity and bought from Germany for a symbolic price 78 biplane fighters B.534 together with other kind of planes like B-71, MB 200 or S-328. In the hangar in the background another Avia fighter biplane is visible. [Courtesy of Stephan Boshniakov]

Junkers Ju 87D-5 of the Bulgarian Air Force. The Stukas were flown by the 1/2 Szturmowi Orliak (assault squadron) [Kagero Archives]

A bad quality but very interesting picture of an Ar.196 flying. This picture was taken in the 50´s, that is the reaso why we can see in the side of the plane, a star. [Courtesy of Stephan Boshniakov]

Another beautiful picture where several D.520 are waiting for the next mission. D.520 was used in many times to attack the bombers while Bf.109s did the same but with the enemy fighters. [Courtesy of Rod´s Warbird]

Manolev, one of the pilots of the four B-135 that on March 30, 1944 took off from the School of Fighter to try to do their best against USAF bombers. [Courtesy of Tod Rathbone, rathbonemuseum.com]

Colonel Valkov, commander of 6th Polk. After the war, in spite of his bravery, he was put under summary trial and then executed. [Picture from Todor Valkov and Courtesy of Tod Rathbone, rathbonemuseum.com]

Several civilians and military personnel close to a newly acquired plane in 1936. In the early 30´s, Bulgaria began to make numerous efforts dedicated to increasing the number of aircraft and therefore air units.
[Courtesy of Tod Rathbone, rathbonemuseum. com]

In this picture we can see the 55th Officer's Graduation class. As a curiosity, several of these men belonged to other Army branches before joining to the Air Force.
[Courtesy of Tod Rathbone, rathbonemuseum.com]

Five Bulgarian pilots pose proudly in this picture. Over their shoulders falled the most part of the Bulgarian efforts in the defence of their air space.
[Courtesy of Tod Rathbone, rathbonemuseum.com]

Five Bulgarian pilots pose proudly in this picture. Onto their shoulders fell the greater part of the Bulgarian efforts in the defence of their air space.
[Picture from Bundesarchiv, Bild 101I-676-7974-13 Keiner CC-BY-SA 3.0]

Close view of the Bulgarian pilot badge, from Bulgharian manufacture.
[Courtesy of Tod Rathbone, rathbonemuseum.com]

Bad quality but very interesting picture of a KB-11. In 1944 50 KB-11 were incorporated in the ranks of the BAF, at that moment fighting against the Germans. This multipurpose plane was one of the most important planes built in Bulgaria. [Courtesy of Stephan Boshniakov]

In this picture we can compare the size of a man in front of a KB-11. From September 1944, the indigenous KB-11s took the place of the PZL.43As that were withdrawn from service in front-line units. The use of the KB-11 before the change of side of Bulgaria consisted mainly of joint reconnaissance flights together the Wehrmacht ground forces and the Bulgarian Army in Serbia against the Tito´s partisan troops. [Courtesy of Stephan Boshniakov]

Several piots and crew pose in front of a KB-11 were we can see the St. Andrew´s Cross badge in the side of the fuselage and the aircraft's numerical codes painted between the national insignia and the tail of the aircraft in white. In the undersurface of the left wing, the numerical code is in dark color. [Courtesy of Stephan Boshniakov]

Picture of a Bulgarian Focke Wulf Fw.58 during maintenance. The 8 copies of this multipurpose plane played different roles in the BAF as transport, liaison, training or light attack plane.
[Courtesy of Stephan Boshniakov]

A pilot equipped for a mission poses for the photographer while he is sitting on the wing of his Bf.109E. We can see the two 20 mm cannons in the wings. [Courtesy of Stephan Boshniakov]

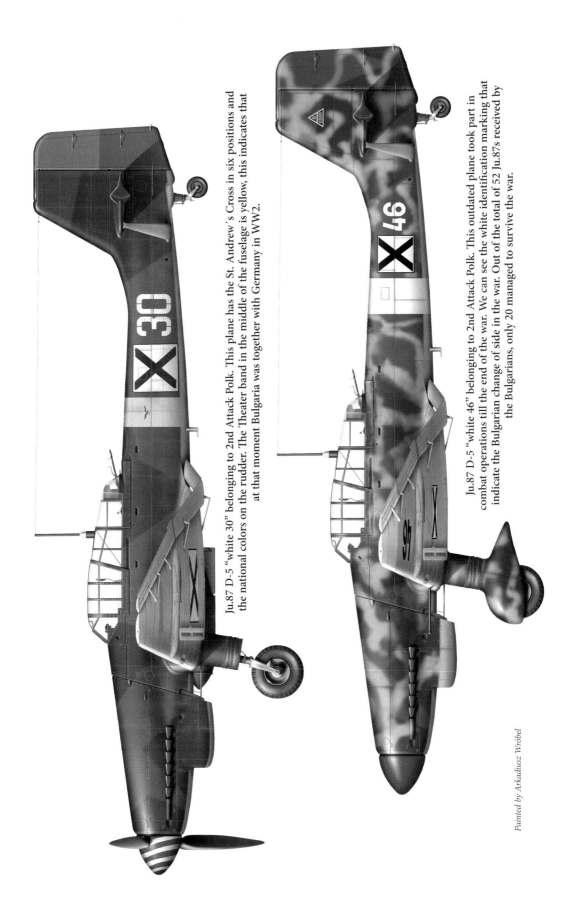

Ju.87 D-5 "white 30" belonging to 2nd Attack Polk. This plane has the St. Andrew's Cross in six positions and the national colors on the rudder. The Theater band in the middle of the fuselage is yellow, this indicates that at that moment Bulgaria was together with Germany in WW2.

Ju.87 D-5 "white 46" belonging to 2nd Attack Polk. This outdated plane took part in combat operations till the end of the war. We can see the white identification marking that indicate the Bulgarian change of side in the war. Out of the total of 52 Ju.87s received by the Bulgarians, only 20 managed to survive the war.

Painted by Arkadiusz Wróbel

Do.17 M-1 "B-G" belonging to 1st Bomber Orlyak. Together with the Do.17 M, 15 ex-Yugoslav Do.17Kb1 bombers were obtained in 1941 as trophies of war. From the aerodrome at Badem Chiflik they were able to carry out maritime surveillance patrols over the Aegean.

Do.17 M-1 belonging to 1st Bomber Orlyak. In 1940 11 Dornier Do.17M (bombers) and P (reconnaissance) were acquired from Germany. One of the last occasions in which the Do 17 M performed bombing missions was on November 12 against German troops in the area of Kachanik.

Painted by Arkadiusz Wróbel

CHAPTER VIII

Maritime Surveillance Units

One of the three spearheads of the BAF together with the fighter and attack forces, were the reconnaissance and maritime attack units. The reason for this branch in BAF was the maintenance of control over seas of Bulgarian sovereignty, which focused on two areas, the Aegean Sea and the waters of the Black Sea. The first one with less enemy activity, due to being far from the combat front, while the second one was continuously subject to the intervention of surface and submarine forces of the Soviet Navy.

One of the first aircraft to participate in these surveillance missions in the Black Sea was the S-328 in units subordinate (along with Romanian aircraft) to the German High Command which was based in Varna.

Although Bulgaria had not declared war on the Soviet Union, unlike the other Axis countries, both Axis ships and Bulgarian ports on the Black Sea were under constant Soviet attack (as Villamor refers). Attack submarines and torpedo boats sowed terror in the convoys that passed through these waters; in addition Bulgarian ports were planted with mines and bombed by the Red aircraft. Therefore, it was necessary to submit to these waters to a tight control that fell to the Bulgarian aviation that also would provide escort to the convoys of the Axis.

These campaigns that took place in the Black Sea and its coastal regions were carried out by Soviet and Axis forces between 1941 and 1944. The maritime campaigns changed according to the development of the war during these four years. Thus, in 1941 Soviet submarines attacked Axis ships in the vicinity of the Romanian and Bulgarian coasts, sinking up to 29,000 tons of ships. In 1943 with the final victory very close, the Soviets had 29 submarines dedicated to operate in the Black Sea; and this increased the Axis armies began their inexorable retreat on the Eastern Front.

As a summary of these campaigns at least 45 Axis ships were sunk (18 Germans, 6 Romanians, 3 Bulgarians, 2 Italians and 16 from neutral Turkey). On the other hand, the Soviets lost up to 28 submarines, in addition to other smaller vessels, in many cases from the effects of minefields on the Rumanian and Bulgarian coasts.

There is no record in the current archives that any Bulgarian aircraft managed to sink an enemy ship or submarine in their surveillance tasks. Although the Russian submarine Shch-204 could have been severely damaged by a Bulgarian aircraft in 1941, it finally sunk after striking a Romanian mine the following day.

Although less important, was the control of the waters close to Turkey and the possible movements that could be spotted there, were always adequately monitored; based on the Bulgarian suspicion that Turkey could at some point position itself in WWII abandoning its neutrality.

Contrary to what one might think at first, the unleashing of "Operation Barbarossa" did not result in a decrease in the Black Sea surveillance forces that the Bulgarians had stationed at their air bases. In fact, the opposite occurred as the number of reconnaissance forces in these waters increased due to the greater danger from the "Soviet Black Sea Fleet" prowling around its maritime control zone (this was motivated by the fact that the German invasion did not really significantly affect Soviet naval power in the Black Sea). The Black Sea airborne surveillance missions departed from the Varna base, from which all maritime control operations were articulated. For these, it was considered appropriate to have seaplanes, as it is advantageous to have the ability to land over the sea during a mission or in case of emergency.

The first aircraft that were used during the war for this purpose were a pair of Heinkel He.42. Soon another aircraft, already used in reconnaissance missions inland, would be added to the two previous models in missions over the Black Sea: the S-328.

Pressed by the request of the Wehrmacht High Command (OK) on July 31, 1941 which required air protection by Bulgaria of German convoys on the Black Sea, on August 4, 1941, a small Bulgarian unit was created and it consisted of four S-328s based in Safarovo (near Burgas on the southern Bulgarian Black Sea coast) and 3-5 aircraft based in Balchik (on the north coast).

Due to the increase of these activities at sea, it was considered necessary to increase the number of aircraft in these missions; it was done by adding 3 more S-328 (being constituted an Orlyak composed of two Yatos of 6 aircraft each). Another important (although outdated for this era) aircraft used in maritime reconnaissance missions was the Heinkel He.60 "Tyulen" (seal), of which it is estimated that in 1942 up to 4 or 5 examples from German surplus were acquired. The He.60s were stationed at Peinerdyik, at Chaika's aircraft base, and integrated into the 161st Coastal Squadron (Yato) of Seaplanes.

These already obsolete aircraft (the S-328 were retired in first line servce from 1942 although they remained in diverse secondary missions until 1944) were giving way to Arado Ar.196 A3, that were acquired from Germany at the beginning of 1943 (having been completely rebuilt and subjected to a perfect set-up). The Germans knew of the importance of controlling that Front that had been opened in the Black

Sea, the reason why on this occasion they did not deprive the Bulgarians of aircraft quite adequate for the reconnaissance missions to realize, as well as with a small capacity of attack and bombardment.

The Ar.196 A3 had two 20 mm MG FF guns on the outside of the wings, a 7.92 mm MG17 machine gun and a 7.92 mm MG15 operated by the observer, as well as being equipped with racks for up to 100 kg of bombs. Its speed reached 310 km/h at 4,000 meters, with a service ceiling of 7,000 m and a range about 1,080 km at 255 km/h. However, they were not equipped with cameras installed on the plane for their reconnaissance missions.

The total of the Ar.196 "Akula" (shark) acquired, amounted to 12 units, which were put into service by June 1943 after a short period of conversion for the crews to the new aircraft. These aircraft had been updated and prepared according to the specifications of the commander of the German naval reconnaissance section (Seeaufklärungsgruppe 125) in the Black Sea located in Varna at the "Bahman" factory in Ribnitz. So they were perfectly prepared for the mission that was to be entrusted to them.

As Nedialkov and Neulen refer, the new aircraft were integrated into the 161st Coastal Squadron (Yato) of Seaplanes located on the Chaika canal (near Varna) under the command of Captain Kolarov and received among other missions the hunt for Russian submarines or make it very difficult for them to act in Bulgarian controlled waters. These aircraft, of which there is currently a specimen with serial number 0219 preserved in the Bulgarian Aviation Museum in Krumovo (near Plovdiv), carried out their combat missions until 1944 when Bulgaria moved onto to the Allied side (by that date Bulgaria had in active service only 8 "Akula"), having from that moment little participation in the war conflict due to the northward withdrawal of Axis forces. After the war they were still active for some years, although with Soviet pressure they had to be withdrawn from service in the late 1940s.

The patrols to be carried out by the aircraft over the Black Sea, had as their main purpose to locate Soviet submarines and if it was possible to attack them with the machine guns and bombs they carried; with the purpose of protecting the Axis convoys. But above all the main thing is that they give a warning signal to Bulgarian ships (as well as Rumanians and Germans) to be on alert to danger, at the same time warning boats and aircraft of the location of the enemy. Other important missions they carried out were the monitoring of mine barriers and other mined areas off the coast near the ports of Varna or Burgas; photo-reconnaissance and rescue missions.

It is estimated that 68 missions carried out by these planes in the Black Sea, of which 41 were convoy escort. In the first years, each convoy was escorted by a single S-328 that when locating a submarine immediately warned the convoy and proceeded to attack with machine gun fire or the small 20 kilogram bombs that the plane carried. The possibility of destroying the submarine was small, but it could well be able to disrupt the action of the Soviets. In addition, as previously mentioned, land based aircraft were alerted to attack them.

The first interception of a submarine occurred on August 16, 1941, when an S-328 plane attacked it as it was prowling in the vicinity of the ships "Tzar Ferdinand" (Bulgarian) and "Cavarna" (Romanian). It was able to drop its bombs and even received the support of three more aircraft (also S-328), although it was not known if the submarine was sunk. On August 30 and September 21 of the same year in two other clashes by S-328 against submarines, the result was equally negative for the Bulgarians. As we can see, the results with the S-328 and its tactics were not working in any way. Although according to some reports on October 15, 1941 an S-328 after dropping its bombs on the Russian submarine M-58, managed to sink it; although it seems more likely that this did not happen as among other reasons the small effect that the small guns and the bombs really had with so little explosive charge that were used.

In spite of the innate work of the different models of aircraft in the control of the Black Sea waters, it is not known that they sank any boats in any of its multiple missions. Although not without merit, it must be recognized that the presence of these aerial observers limited in some way the ease that Soviets could have in attacking the Axis flotillas because its continuous tracking of the sea. It is noteworthy in this regard, in spite of not having sunk any boat in these waters, that an airplane that could have been very valid for coastal anti-ship and anti-submarine missions like the Ju.87 was never used in this type of mission. It is true that it was basically engaged in anti-partisan tasks, but it would certainly have given the Bulgarians a greater firepower and improved odds of actually striking the enemy.

As a last point to be highlighted is the fact that when referring to coastal surveillance, we have always referred to the Black Sea coast, leaving completely Aegean waters under Bulgarian control. For this reason it is necessary to write several words about this matter.

As early as late April 1941, when Bulgarian forces took possession of their new territories in Macedonia and Thrace, air reconnaissance units were deployed to the coastal areas with the task of controlling the Aegean waters tracking the possible precense of enemy ships. It is not known if Bulgarian seaplanes carried out surveillance tasks in these waters, which were already much quieter due to the absence of an enemy as close as it was to the Black Sea with the Soviets always prowling. In addition, the outreach and the existence of the European continental part of Turkey between the two Bulgarian maritime areas of control did not allow the planes in one theatre to act easily in the other (remember that the main base was in Varna). This is why coastal surveillance missions and anti-submarine patrols were carried out by other types of aircraft such as B-71s or Do.17Ms. Since the end of April 1941, as discussed above, after the occupation of its new territories in Greece and Yugoslavia some air units were moved to new aerodromes in those lands. And so on June 26, 1941, when 6 B-71 and 9 Do.17M were transferred to their new operational base at the Badem Chiflik aerodrome near the Greek coastal city of Kavala. From there the operational range of these aircraft was exploited to the maximum, being able to reach any area of the Aegean Sea to support the Axis (in this case mainly Italian) ships.

Principle seaplanes (according mr. Nedialkov source)

Name	Nickname	Number	Year of arrival	Origin	Armament	Engine
Arado Ar.196 (two crew)	Akula (Shark)	12	1943	Germany	Two 20mm cannons and two 7.92 mm machine guns + 100 kg bombs	radial BMW 9 cylinders 132K 960 HP
Heinkel He.42 (two crew biplane)	Patitza or Patica (Duck)	2	1940	Germany	–	Junkers L5G 296 HP
Heinkel He.60 (two crew biplane)	Tyulen (Seal)	2 2	1942 1943	Germany	Two 7.92 mm machine guns	BMW VI 6.0 2U 660 HP

CHAPTER IX

Transport Units

The participation of the different transport units of the Air Force of Bulgaria was small, being limited to carry out its tasks within the territory of Bulgaria and the areas annexed during the conflict. Indeed, if the preparation of the fighter and bombing branches of the air forces had left much to be desired, as far as transport was concerned the situation was even worse. An adequate and effective transport force had not been planned, which as we shall see below, was based on the use of only two "modern" aircraft for this purpose, as they were Ju.52.

The main workhorse therefore consisted of the small fleet of Junkers Ju.52 from which the Bulgarians were able to use. The nickname by which these aircraft were known was "Sova" (owl).

As early as 1938, two Ju.52/3mg6e were acquired from the Junkers factory that would carry the registrations LZ-UNA and LZ-UNB respectively. We have to remember that the role played by Bulgaria during WWII was completely limited because of its circumscription to a geographical location as solid as was Great Bulgaria, which as in other branches of the Air Force determined that the German ally did not provide adequately or in number or as new aircraft. This meant that it was necessary to wait for 5 years more, in 1943 for two new Ju.52/3m to join the transport fleet.

One of the tasks assumed by Ju.52 was to be used by the parachutists of the battalion "Drujina" that had been created on July 1, 1943 as a unit. Due to the importance given to these, they were offered the possibility of using the old-fashioned but reliable "Sova". These were also supplemented by a technical service for aircraft and for aerodromes (two Krilos respectively).

Already after the Coup d´état in Bulgaria, one more was seized from the Luftwaffe in Serbia in 1944 and several more that amounted to a total of 7, at the aerodrome of Zeltweg in Austria in May of 1945.

During the months that the Bulgarians fought against the Germans, the bulk of the transport operations were carried by Ju.52/3m, and it is known that they carried out several transport missions in support of the 1st Army.

The great value of Ju.52 for the Bulgarians was demonstrated by their maintenance in active service despite the great desire of the Soviets after the WWII to eliminate any material of German origin in their satellite countries. Two of them were integrated into the Air Transport Directory in 1947 (these with serials LZ-UNL and LZ-UNO), 6 being in service by 1949, to be finally retired in 1960.

Another plane used as a light transport was one Caudron 440 of French origin, which had to be returned; as well as a Junkers W.34 (nicknamed Darvenitza by the Bulgarians) that was captured from the Germans after the change of side of the Bulgarians in September 1944 to carry out missions against its old owners before its later crash in July of 1945 in Pech (Hungary).

In addition to a fleet of outdated aircraft of little value in the transport role, other aircraft that were also used in transporting personnel and materials in Bulgaria with the best performance were two Junkers F.13, a Focke-Wulf A. 20 "Roselius" (donated by a German commercial representative in Bulgaria) and an He.111 that was dedicated to transport tasks from the first moment it joined the Bulgarian aviation. About the He.111H16, Bulgaria had two aircraft since 1943 that accomplished transport and VIP transport tasks. The Heinkels used civilian registration although they were armed for defence purpose. At the end of the war, both He.111 were "donated" to the Czechoslovakian Air Force.

It is important to remember that in the BAF, several aircraft changed their role as they became outdated, one example was the Do.11 bomber which acted as a transport since the beginning of the hostilities, since evidently as a bomber it could do little in the European skies of the early 40's.

The main airbase for the transport aircraft was Vrazhdebna, close to Sofia (nowadays corresponding to the airport of Sofia). In addition, a number of minor aerodromes were naturally used in their operational travels both in Bulgaria and in the newly incorporated territories in Thrace, Macedonia and South Dobruja. In spite of this, always due to the scarce and mainly inadequate transport fleet, its activity could not have the importance that would have required especially in the continuous internal war that was maintained against the partisans. This fact helped to a certain extent that the bulk of these anti-partisan operations were carried out by the German troops.

Principle transport planes (according mr. Nedialkov source)

Name	Nickname	Number	Year of arrival	Origin	Armament	Engine
Junkers Ju.52/3m (five crew)	Sova (Owl)	7 (¿+5?)	1938-43-44	Germany	2 7.92 mm machine guns	3 x BMW 132T 830 HP
Heinkel He.111H16 (four crew)	–	2	1943	Germany	Up to 7 7.92 mm machine gun + 1 20 mm cannon	2 x Jumo 211 F-2 1300 HP
Junkers W.34	Darvenitza	1	1933	Germany	300 kg bombs	BMW 132 660 HP

CHAPTER X

Bulgarian Aviation Insignia

The BAF badges varied throughout the years immediately prior to and during the conflict. Before 1940 (from 1937), the emblem used was the one that represented the Bulgarian medal for Bravery, that consisted of a red cross of Malta crossed by two swords and with a white and red circle in the center where a golden lion was placed.

From 1940 and because of its alliance with Germany, the badges were modified to become a diagonal cross in black on a white square background with black border (similar to the cross of Saint Andrew used in the Air Force of Spain). During this period, the aircraft's numerical codes were painted on the fuselage, between the national insignia and the tail of the aircraft, usually in white or black with a white trim.

Later with the restructurings realized in the BAF, in an Orlyak the planes of the Headquarter would carry their numbers in yellow; those of the first Yato would be white, those of the second green and those of the third red.

Also because of the participation of the BAF in intercepting the missions of the Allied bombers, they adopted the same system of tactical identification as that used by the Luftwaffe that was to paint the tips of the wings a yellow color and a band on the tail of the planes.

After the Coup d´état in September of 1944, the emblem of the cross remained in the first case, although a new element was applied to demonstrate the property of the airplane to the new anti-German Bulgarian government. This consisted of a white band 75 cm wide on the fuselage and the tips of the wings. As an example, the Ar.196 used green toned liveries with yellow under the wingtips (as corresponded to the eastern front) until Bulgaria changed side when they replaced yellow with white. These marks of identification would last until March of 1945.

Finally in January 1945 with the change of commander-in-chief of the Air Forces, which would now be General Gancho Manchev and the beginning of the restructuring of the same following Soviet guidelines, the national emblem was again modified, now consisting in a circle of white and red with a green line crossing it.

CHAPTER XI

Aerial Victory Scoring System of the BAF And Aces

The system of scoring aerial victories during the Second World War varied among the different countries. In Bulgaria the victory score stipulated by the General Staff of the BAF was used up to March 18, 1944. This order stipulated the awarding of points to the pilots as follows:

– 3 points: for shooting down a 4-engined bomber or for shooting down a single four-engined plane not previously damaged.

– 2 points: for damaging a four-engined plane; for the destruction of a twin-engined bomber; for shooting down a previously undamaged twin-engined bomber or for damaging a twin-engined bomber.

– 1 point: for shooting down a four-engined bomber previously damaged or for shooting down a fighter.

Damaging a fighter was not acknowledged with the award of any points.

In this way, the classification of the seven main Bulgarian fighter pilots (or aces as they are commonly called) remained as follows:

Name	Victories	Damaged	Points	Unit
Stoyan Stoyanov	4	5	15	682nd Yato 3/6
Petar Bochev	4	3	13	3/6
Chudomir Toplodolski	4	2	8	3/6 HQ
Gencho Dimitrov	3	2	7	692nd Yato 3/6
Nedelcho Bonchev	3	1	9	652nd Yato 2/6
Ivan Bonev	3	1	8	682nd Yato 3/6
Marin Tzvetkov	2	5	10	672nd Yato 3/6

These data are based on those of Teodor Muchovski collected in the work of Jan J. Safarik, and can be considered as accurate as possible at present as far as the BAF are concerned. Despite this, checking other sources always shows a small variation of figures, because of the complication that actually results in the confirmation of shot down, as well as some authors who increase the figures. Finally, it is necessary to remember that there are pilots who having small number of shoot downs can have more points than other pilots, simply because of the type of plane attacked and the number of damaged aircraft that they obtained.

CHAPTER XII

Rank Equivalents In The Bulgarian Air Force

During WW2 the ranks that used the members of the BAF according to Thomas, Mikulan and Mollo were:

Bulgarian	English
Rednik	Private
Efreytor	Lance-corporal
Kandidat Podofitser	Corporal
Podofitser	Sergeant
Feldfebel	Warrant Officer
Ofiserski Kandidat	Junior 2nd Lieutenant
Podporuchik	2nd Lieutenant
Poruchik	Lieutenant
Kapitan	Captain
Mayor	Major
Podpolkovnik	Lieutenant Colonel
Polkovnik	Colonel
General-Mayor	Major-General
General-Leytenant	Lieutenant-General
General	General
Marshal	Field-Marshal

Conclusion

After narrating the difficult times that the BAF lived through during World War II, and its dedication to the defense of its country despite the many adversities, we must appreciate the great courage and spirit of combat that demonstrated the BAF pilots, so much in the pro-Axis period as in their pro-Allied period.

At the beginning of World War II Bulgaria found itself in the side of Germany and although it was a peaceful period for the country, the BAF was used against partisan troops mainly in occupied territories. When the American giant appeared over Bulgaria, the pilots and ground staff did their best to achieve that their Air Force faced Allied bombers and escort fighters in an unequal struggle in which they always encountered numerical and technological inferiority. After the change of side, Bulgaria had to fight against Germany, wounded but still not defeated. Under the command of USSR HQ, they were used as cannon fodder with their battered and sometimes old planes against their former German allies.

For these reasons and despite the limited knowlege of their participation in the Second World conflict, it is fair to pay tribute to them with this text that has tried to make its history become better known.

Bibliography

Angelucci, Enzo; Matricardi, Paolo, Pinto, Pierluigi. " Complete book of World War II Combat Aircraft". White Star Publishers. 2001.

Belcarz, Bartlomiej; Alexandrov, Krasimir. "Dewoitine D.520". Mushroom Model Publications. 2005.

Bily, Miroslav. "Avia B-35 B-135" . MBI. 2003.

Franks, RA. The Focke-Wulf Fw 189 Uhu. Valiant Wings. 2015.

Glass, Andrzej. "PZL P.24 A-G". Kagero. 2004.

Holmes, Tony. "Jane´s Pocket Guide Fighters of World War II". Harpers Collings Publishing. 1999.

Karnas, Dariusz. "Fieseler Fi 156 Storch 1933–1945". Mushroom Model Publications. 2012.

Kopanski, Tomasz J. "PZL P.23 Karas". Mushroom Model Publications. 2004.

Kudlicka, Bohumil. "Avia B-534. Czechoslovakian fighter 1933-45". Czechs Master´s Kits Photo Hobby. 2006.

Mollo, A. The armed forces of World War II. Greenwich Editions. 2000.

Mondey, David. "The Hamlyn Concise Guide to Axis Aircraft of World War II". Chancellor Press. 1984.

Murawski, M. Arado Ar 196. Kagero. 2011.

Murawski, M. Dornier Do17/Do215. Kagero. 2015.

Murawski, M; Plewka, J. Messerschmitt f 109 E. The Blitzkrieg fighter. Kagero. 2013.

Nedialkov, Dimitar. "Air power of the kingdom of Bulgaria part III". FARK ODD. 2001.

Nedialkov, Dimitar. "Air power of the kingdom of Bulgaria part IV". FARK ODD. 2001.

Nedialkov, Dimitar. "Bulgarian fighters part I". "Propeller" Publishing. 2006.

Nedialkov, Dimitar. "Bulgarian fighters part II". "Propeller" Publishing. 2006.

Neulen, Hans Werner. "In the skies of Europe". The Crowood Press. 2000.

Peczkowski, Robert. "Messerschmitt Bg-109G". Mushroom Model Publications. 2000.

Punka, G. Focke-Wulf Fw 189 in action. Squadron Signal. 1993.

Rajlich, Jiri; Boshniakov, Stephen; Mandjukov, Petko. "Slovakian and Bulgarian aces of war world 2". Osprey Publishing. 2004.

Safarik, Jan, "Bulgaria. The air combats and the victories of the Bulgarian fighters". 2008.

Stapfer, Hans-Heiri. "Tupolev SB in action". Squadron Signal. 2004.

Thomas, N; Mikulin, K. Axis forces in Yugoslavia 1941–1945. Osprey. 1995.

Villamor, R. La batalla del Kubán 1943. Almena. 2017.

Vrany, Jiri. " Letov S-328. Vol 2". Jakab. 2005.

Volkov, Todor. The Story of the Bulgarian Air Force up to 9 September 1944.

Wawrzynski, Miroslav. "Ju 87 in foreign service". Mushroom Model Publications. 2005.

www. Wikipedia.org

www.aeroflight.co.uk/waf/bulgaria

www.ariergard.net/index.php?option=com_content&view=article&id=123:-a-brief-history-of-the-bulgarian-military-aviation-during-the-two-world-wars&catid=50:articles&Itemid=69

www.armchairgeneral.com/bulgaria-in-world-war-ii.htm

www.asisbiz.com

www.bibliotekata.wordpress.com

www.exordio.com/1939–1945/paises/bulgaria.html

www.forum.axishistory.com/

www.guerra-abierta.blogspot.com.es/2011/10/real-fuerza-aerea-bulgara-1939-1944-y.html7

www.modelingmadness.com/review/preww2

www.niehorster.orbat.com/032_bulgaria/_aircraft.html

www.sofiaecho.com/2011/01/21/1028646_bombing-sofia

www. rathbonemuseum.com

www.vojska.net/eng/world-war-2/bulgaria/
www.warbirdphotographs.com/
www.ww2aircraft.net/forum/aircraft-pictures/bulgarian-air-force-27996-2.html
www.ww2aircraft.net/forum/aircraft-pictures/bulgarian-air-force-27996-5.html
www.ww2fighters.e-monsite.com/pages/content/dewoitine-d-520-5.html
www.www.eurasia1945.com/batallas/contienda/invasion-de-yugoslavia/